SPIRITUAL & PRACTICAL STEPS
TO
COMMANDING
VALUE

How to package your business (skills & talent) in a way that
will command maximum value in the Marketplace.

Principles of Strategic Positioning for Success in the New Economy
& How to develop your Personal Brand for Exceptional Increase.

Charles Omole
Author of " Understanding Dominion"

Content

*This book is dedicated to all the
Champions of Faith in the secular arena…
it is time to command value and show the
world your true worth as we begin to
strategically reclaim the marketplace.
Go and occupy.*

Introduction

Value is what life is about. People respond to things and people based on their perceived value. What people pay you for your service is based on the value they place on you. That is why two people can be doing the same job and get paid miles apart. But for some Christians; there is an added complication. Many folks in Church carry the "Spirituality" thing too far. They think the fact that God has anointed them is enough for them to command value.

My mission in this book is to show you through scriptures that you must translate your giftings into the language of value. Joseph was anointed we all agree about that. Yet he had to change his appearance when Pharaoh called on him. He shaved, he changed his clothes…why? Why did he not just rely on his anointing? He realised rightly that in the Marketplace; you have to speak their language of value to command value. Later on Apostle Paul stated in the New Testament that he had to become all things to all men that he may win some. (1 Corinthians 9: 19-22) That is what I call adaptive Christianity…which is largely lacking today. As our destiny is to reclaim the Marketplace for the Lord' we need to get out of the church-mindset and embrace the variations of opportunity God has created to show forth the grace and anointing He has placed in us.

> *"A poor, wise man knew how to save the town, and so it was rescued. But afterward **no one** seriously thought **to thank him**. So even though wisdom is better than strength, those who are wise will be despised if they are poor. **What they say** will not be **appreciated** for long".*
>
> Ecclesiastes 9:15-16 (NLT)

You are gifted. You are talented. You have unique skills and competencies. You are an inventor. Or you have started a new business? Why is it that you are the most qualified in your office but yet you are the least paid? Why are people not willing to pay for your gift, talents and skills? The Bible says the wisdom of a poor man is not valued; even though his wisdom rescued the city. So how do you package your business (skills & talent) in a way that will command maximum value? How do you package your gifting in ways that will make people be willing to pay a premium for it? Being gifted is not enough; you have to be seen as gifted by the people that will pay for your gift in the Marketplace. That is what commanding value is all about.

The truth is you are not really paid in life for your talent, skill or time...you are paid for your Value. Poor man's one hour is the same as Rich man's one hour; but the value of the individual is different. Why do two people with the same skill get paid differently? Why are two businesses offering the same services get different patronage? Why do people walk pass you to go and pay big money to your competitor, to do what you are more than able to do.

> *"You are the light of the world. A city that is set on a hill cannot be hidden. Nor do they light a lamp and put it under a basket, but on a lampstand, and it gives light to all who are in the house."*
>
> - Matthew 5:14-15

The global economy is changing and old tools and systems will not work in the new emerging Marketplace. How do you strategically position yourself, your career, your business and your ministry for what is about to explode in the Nations.

In this exciting new book; we will be looking at issues like; Biblical Principles of Strategic Positioning in the Marketplace, Strategies on Developing a Personal Brand of Yourself or Ministry, Developing and enhancing your Career Prospect in economic downturn, Generating Business Ideas, Strategies on Increasing & Promoting the Value of your Gift and many more. This book will change your life for the better forever. That much I can guarantee. God has done His part by anointing you; its time that you do your part by making that investment relevant and valuable to others in ways that will extend the frontiers of God's Kingdom.

In this book, you will learn the steps and strategies to package your gift in the language of Value. You will be taught the secret of increasing your Value and consequently increase your income. This is a Bible-based book; I make no apologies for that. This is not a book on marketing, branding or public relations. Any principle you find in these fields of study in this book are only incidental to illustrate valid Biblical doctrines.

So whether you are working for an employer or you manage your own business; you will learn how to command the greatest value and attract maximum return. Your life, business, ministry will never remain the same. I congratulate you as you are about to be promoted to the next level in God. It is well with you. Amen!

Charles Omole

CHAPTER 1

Understanding
The Spiritual Foundation

"Then the seventh angel sounded: And there were loud voices in heaven, saying, "The kingdoms[a] of this world have become the kingdoms of our Lord and of His Christ, and He shall reign forever and ever!".

Rev 11:15

"And it shall come to pass in the last days, that the mountain of the LORD's house shall be established in the top of the mountains, and shall be exalted above the hills; and all nations shall flow unto it. And many people shall go and say, Come ye, and let us go up to the mountain of the LORD, to the house of the God of Jacob; and he will teach us of his ways, and we will walk in his paths: for out of Zion shall go forth the law, and

the word of the LORD from Jerusalem ".
Isaiah 2: 2 – 4

A closer look at these two scriptures reveals some fundamental realities that will affect all believers in these last days. Firstly, the bible says the kingdom of this world will become the kingdom of our Lord and His Christ. It means that there will be a kingdom collision. One kingdom is going to absorb another. Some will call it wealth transfer. It means what currently is being controlled by the gentiles (or perhaps enemy) would be transferred to believers. So we know that there will be a kingdom takeover.

But how is that going to happen? Isaiah 2 says *"And it shall come to pass in the last days that the mountain of god's house shall be exalted above all mountains".* It means that there will be other mountains but the one of the Lord shall be exalted above all. This is of key importance. Scripture states that the people who are not of the Lord will say; let us all go into the house of the Lord that they may teach us their ways.

Now that means the kingdom takeover will not be solely by forceful imposition. There is a substantial element of submission to what they have seen. Which means that the kingdom takeover that is going to happen is not just going to be about taking it by force from them only, but they will be compelled to submit by seeing the excellence with which the Church is operating. Can you remember when the queen of Sheba went to see Solomon? The bible says she entered Solomon's house, she saw orderliness of the house of Solomon, she saw the gold cutlery, she was so mesmerized by what she saw and the bible says her legs could no longer carry her. Which meant that she saw the excellence being displayed by Solomon that she even, (that she thought she came from an excellent background) had to submit to superior excellence.

So there is a dimension of the wealth transfer that will take place that will not just be by forceful imposition but by the church developing certain strategies and values that others will look at and say "...wow you know what, I want what they have.." That is what the bible is saying in Isaiah chapter two. It says "And they will say of their own free will, let us go into the house of the Lord, that they may teach us (not their doctrines), that they may teach us their ways. But for that to happen, we need to understand the value of what we carry as children of God. And I think that is a challenge generally for the church. We don't understand the value of what we have in Christ as we should. Now we can't begin to talk about this without understanding the principle of Tyre and Sidon.

Now if you look at Ezekiel 27; the whole chapter is dedicated to two cities, Tyre and Sidon. Now the Bible makes it clear in Ezekiel 26 and 27 that there is no manner of trade or business you are looking for that you will not find in Tyre and Sidon. Hence it meant therefore that Tyre and Sidon became the representation of the marketplace. So whoever controls Tyre and Sidon controls the marketplace. And whoever control the marketplace, controls the destiny of nations.

So God now told Ezekiel in chapter 28, to do two things; to make a proclamation and a lamentation. The first one is against the Prince of Tyre from Ezekiel 28 vs 1 and then from verse 11 to make a proclamation against the King of Tyre. Now we need to understand the difference between those two personalities so that as we proceed we begin to decode the spiritual operations of the Marketplace.

> *"The word of the LORD came again unto me, saying, ² Son of man, say unto the prince of Tyre, Thus saith the Lord GOD; Because thine heart is lifted up, and thou hast said, I am a God, I sit in the seat of God, in the midst of the seas; yet thou art a man, and not God, though thou set thine heart as the heart of God: ³ Behold, thou art wiser than Daniel; there is no secret that they can hide from thee: ⁴ With thy wisdom and with thine*

understanding thou hast gotten thee riches, and hast gotten gold and silver into thy treasures: [5] *By thy great wisdom and by thy traffick hast thou increased thy riches, and thine heart is lifted up because of thy riches:* [6] *Therefore thus saith the Lord GOD; Because thou hast set thine heart as the heart of God;* [7] *Behold, therefore I will bring strangers upon thee, the terrible of the nations: and they shall draw their swords against the beauty of thy wisdom, and they shall defile thy brightness.* [8] *They shall bring thee down to the pit, and thou shalt die the deaths of them that are slain in the midst of the seas.* [9] *Wilt thou yet say before him that slayeth thee, I am God? but thou shalt be a man, and no God, in the hand of him that slayeth thee.* [10] *Thou shalt die the deaths of the uncircumcised by the hand of strangers: for I have spoken it, saith the Lord GOD.*

Ezekiel 28:1-10

While examining the twin cities of Tyre and Sidon, we need to understand the principles involved. From verse one of Ezekiel 28 the Bible tells us that the word of the Lord came to Ezekiel saying "*son of man, say to the prince of Tyre thus says the Lord God, because your heart is lifted up, and you say I am God, I seat in the seat of God in the midst of the seas and yet you are a man and not a god*". That instantly means that the prince of Tyre is a human being like you and I. We can also see from verses 2 to 10 of Ezekiel 28 that the prince of Tyre is a human being that is; somebody you can see face to face.

After he made that declaration, God told him that I now need you to make a lamentation from verse 11 against the king of Tyre. But who is the king of Tyre? As with any kingdom we know; the real decision maker and ultimate power is the King. So the prince can only function to the extent that the King gives him power to. Accordingly the real decision maker is the King and not the Prince. So who is this King of Tyre that spiritually control the Marketplace?

> [11] *Moreover the word of the LORD came unto me, saying,* [12] *Son of man, take up a lamentation upon the king of Tyre, and say unto him, Thus saith the Lord GOD; Thou sealest up the sum, full of wisdom, and perfect in beauty.* [13] *Thou hast been in Eden the garden of God; every precious stone was thy covering, the sardius, topaz, and the diamond, the beryl, the onyx, and the jasper, the sapphire, the emerald, and the carbuncle, and gold: the workmanship of thy tabrets and of thy pipes was prepared in thee in the day that thou wast created.* [14] *Thou art the*

anointed cherub that covereth; and I have set thee so: thou wast upon the holy mountain of God; thou hast walked up and down in the midst of the stones of fire. [15] Thou wast perfect in thy ways from the day that thou wast created, till iniquity was found in thee. [16] By the multitude of thy merchandise they have filled the midst of thee with violence, and thou hast sinned: therefore I will cast thee as profane out of the mountain of God: and I will destroy thee, O covering cherub, from the midst of the stones of fire.

[17] Thine heart was lifted up because of thy beauty, thou hast corrupted thy wisdom by reason of thy brightness: I will cast thee to the ground, I will lay thee before kings, that they may behold thee. [18] Thou hast defiled thy sanctuaries by the multitude of thine iniquities, by the iniquity of thy traffick; therefore will I bring forth a fire from the midst of thee, it shall devour thee, and I will bring thee to ashes upon the earth in the sight of all them that behold thee. [19] All they that know thee among the people shall be astonished at thee: thou shalt be a terror, and never shalt thou be any more.

Ezekiel 28:11-19

Remember verses 1 to 10 was about the prince of Tyre and from verse 11 is the king of Tyre. The Bible stated *"...you are the seal of perfections, full of wisdom and perfect in beauty. You are in Eden the garden of God and every precious stone was your covering, the sardius, topaz and the diamond, the beryl, the onyx, the jasper, the sapphire, the emerald and the carbuncle, and gold, the workmanship of your timbrels and of your pipes was prepared for you on the day you were created. You were the anointed cherub covers... I establish you. You are on the holy mountain of God. You walked back and forth in the midst of the stone you are perfect in your ways from the day you were created until iniquity was found in you..."* So who is the king of Tyre? Satan is the King of Tyre.

Now, read this carefully, the prince of Tyre is a human being you see face to face in the marketplace. Who is the prince of Tyre? Anyone that is not born-again is the prince of Tyre. Nature abhors vacuum so if you are not under the influence of God you must be under the influence of Satan. So anyone you see, your boss, your partner, your colleague; anyone in your workplace that you see around, depending on the spirit operating in them, are either princes of Tyre or princes of God. The real controller of the marketplace is the king of Tyre. Now we see that the king of Tyre is the real controller and the prince of Tyre is just a human being that is being used. Why? Because when God created the earth; He declared that the only person that can operate legally in it is somebody born of a woman. Satan knows that, therefore he knows that he cannot operate freely without human helpers (Princes).

So Satan influences people and he uses people to achieve his objective. The Prince is a physical ruler over Tyre and Sidon and the King is the spiritual ruler. The physical ruler is who you see but the spiritual ruler is the one pressing the buttons. So we know that the physical ruler is not really your enemy, it is the spiritual one that is your enemy. When there is an issue rather than struggling with the physical ruler, you need to go to where it matters and dislodge the spiritual ruler. Suddenly, the physical ruler becomes easy to deal with.

Therefore the people that are opposing you in the marketplace are doing so, not by themselves, but under the influence of the King of Tyre. It is the king of Tyre that is using them to oppose you. Therefore, if you now descend into flesh and blood   fighting, you have missed the point all together. Because it is not about somebody does not like you, he is not signing you promotion letter, and he is not doing this and that; all that is not the issue. The issue is, who is controlling that person? And until you understand that there is a spiritual warfare that you are fighting in the marketplace, you will not succeed.

A good example was a personal situation a few years ago. I just came back from a trip to the US and my wife (on my return home) gave me a piece of paper, on it she had written a petition, complaining that her boss at work was making her life hellish. And she believes it is racially motivated and so she had written a petition which she wanted me to proof read. I said ah! Me proof read petition? I knew instantly that was not the way to handle this. So I sat her down and explained Ezekiel 28 to her that if you write a petition, who are you going to give it to? She said their overall boss. I said you are trying to judge a prince of Tyre; and you are giving another prince of Tyre the opportunity to adjudicate. What type of judgment will you get? I said no, we have to deal with this in a different way. So I asked for the name of her manager at work; and I took the case to the Throne Room of God. About a week later she came back and said, guess what happened? I said what? She said that their overall boss came to their office and told her manager (the one giving her stress) that there is a position in another division and that he (the overall boss) had already volunteered this manager for that assignment. My wife's troublesome manager insisted she did not apply for a transfer; but the overall boss said he had already applied on her behalf and she must resume in the new division that same day. That day was the day the woman stopped being my wife's manager.

I now asked my wife, *"how long did you think your petition would have taken you?"* She was ecstatic and that was the end of her problem at work. I dealt with the issue where it matters; rather than resort to fleshly means. Sadly many believers tend to begin to fight and struggle and by the time we are fighting in the flesh, we are fighting with the weapons the enemy control. But if you fight through divine means, Satan does not know what to do with you. It is therefore important for you to understand then that when you are being opposed physically by people, it is not them. The devil will not stand physically in front of you to oppose you, he is not allowed to. Why, because the Lord has pronounced it so; that only a person born of a woman can legally operate here on earth. He can't appear in the devilish form in that sense. He must always operate through people.

I have my own business outfits I manage and truth is if you are eating from the scrap and you are doing menial jobs then the enemy may probably leave you alone. But as you begin to climb up in the marketplace, you begin to encounter more resistance, in all manner or forms. You need to know how to deal with them, because if you deal with them in the flesh, you will never win. You need to understand therefore, that our battle is primarily spiritual. The marketplace is a spiritual entity, which we cannot just dabble into anyhow.

I read somewhere a while ago that the rate of business failure in the Christian community is the highest. Why? Because our people stumble into business thinking it is about business plan, some academic degrees they have and the formula they have, but they quickly realize that it is not as easy because Satan will   make sure it is not easy for them. Because you know that once you are a child of God, the devil has your number. It is not in his interest to make it easy for you.

The Bible says in the book of Hebrew that *"the children of Israel walked on the red sea as unto dry land. But when the Egyptians tried to do the same, they drowned"*.

> *'our people stumble into business thinking it is about business plan, some academic degrees they have and the formula they have, but they quickly realize that it is not as easy because Satan will   make sure it is not easy for them'*

Now what does that mean? It means that there is a technology God revealed to his own people, but that technology worked only on the platform of relationship. So those who see what you do and try to copy the same thing it would not work for them even though they are doing exact same thing you are doing. Why? Because they don't have relationship that will create the platform or the enabling environment and grace for that thing to work. Similarly, it works with the enemy too in that he will make certain things in the marketplace easier for his own people but will raise strong opposition against the child of God. Hence the need for spiritual warfare.

You observe an unbeliever doing something wrong for ten years and was never caught. So you decided to do same. But you do it once and you are caught. Satan will use every tool he has to fight a believer; so we have an enemy that is involved in a battle that has no ceasefire. Why are many believers the most qualified in their work places yet they are the least paid. Their bosses don't have ten percent of their qualifications. This simply means the battle is not for the strong and it is the favour of God that distinguishes us.

We cannot fight the battle of reclaiming the marketplace using the weapons controlled by the enemy. Because for every educational certificate you bring to the marketplace, the enemy will bring five more people with same or better certificates than you do. So you can't win on that basis. You put the best business plan together and you don't get the funds and somebody walks in without a business plan at all and he gets it. It means therefore remembering what the bible says that the battle is not for the strong you now begin to see that favour is what distinguishes you. So it's important that as we begin to look at how the marketplace operates, that we begin to fine-tune our strategies as believers. Remember we are looking at the subject of commanding value.

> *"We cannot fight the battle of reclaiming the marketplace using the weapons controlled by the enemy"*

How do you command value? Clearly, a rich man's one hour is the same as the poor man's one hour. An hour has 60 minutes so in life you are not paid for your time, but for your value. Rich men don't have the duration of their seconds different, it is the same thing. Their clocks are exactly the same in terms of time and duration. But they would make in one hour what some people cannot make in a year. When you hear a footballer makes three hundred thousand pounds a week, you begin to imagine that most people make less than that in a week; although the duration of a week is same for all. Also we need to begin to see that money is not about cash. The moment you think money is about cash, you are already poor instantly.

CHAPTER 2

Understanding
Value Definition

Τhis is not a book on Marketing; so the traditional understanding of value proposition will not strictly apply. I am borrowing the word 'Value' in order to illustrate general principles that govern the strategic invasion of the Marketplace by the Church of God. So permit me if I accentuate only a narrow definition to boost my approach.

God wants us to think big. There is a difference between thinking survival, (about your personal issues, and family); and thinking about the Kingdom. Sometimes in 2011; I was at a top business meeting in London and I was given the profile of about sixty to seventy people who were in the room. And the least among them earns two hundred thousand pounds per annum. As I picked up the microphone to speak, the first thing I said (I don't know where it came from, it was not in my notes) was *"...Hmmm, it's a pity I am in a room full of poor people".* And instantly you could see all of them looking at me wondering if I had read their profiles. I stated that I had read their profiles and I know that the least among them earns two hundred thousand pounds per annum. But all of you are still poor people, I declared.

And I explained further, that if you are looking at it from the perspective of what you will eat, the house you will live, the car you will drive – just you and your family, if you are on two hundred thousand pounds per annum, then you are probably ok. Because for your personal needs that is ok. But I said if they understand that Saturday evening Prime Time one minute advert can cost as much as £70,000; which means their entire annual salary cannot pay for God to be preached for 3minutes on main TV. I made them to see how poor they really are, when it comes to the Kingdom? In the US they have this game called 'The Super Bowl'. It happens once a year. Adverts on that day go as far as $10Million for one minute, because two thirds of American viewing audience watch super ball. Can you imagine you if you can preach the gospel to such large audience? What impact it will have on the nation.

The moment you begin to look at things from the kingdom perspective, you start to see what many consider as rich is nothing. That is why the Bible says in Zachariah that my city's true prosperity shall yet be established. We need to begin to think beyond our personal financial comfort alone and see that the Kingdom should be the overriding priority. I call it going beyond Rehoboth. Many of us have seen lots of Rehoboth conferences and there is nothing wrong with Rehoboth by the way. But it looks as if we all close our Bibles after the verse on Rehoboth. But if you continue reading in Genesis 26 you find that Isaac dug one more well after Rehoboth. There is a journey beyond Rehoboth. For a truth; you have not yet won and taken over the marketplace until you move beyond Rehoboth.

Yes the Lord has made room for you in the land, but you have still not taken over the marketplace until you dig one more well Isaac called Sheba. If you read Genesis chapter 26 from verse 22 to 32 you will see that when he dug the final well at Sheba, that is actually when he took over. Because the people of the land now came to submit to him fully. So it is important therefore that we understand as believers that the series of little victories that we enjoy should not be seen as the end of it all.

Part of the challenge with the church is that God gives some of us a little bit of headway and many will even disappear from church altogether. Once we make a little money, the church is no longer relevant. With little bits and pieces we see, we begin to take it as though that is the end not knowing that it is just the beginning of the journey into abundance. You have not really won until you win in the marketplace. So many of us have been stopping at Rehoboth. Rehoboth was achieved without successful engagement of the people of the land. Rehoboth is the place of becoming successful. But beyond Rehoboth, that is where you find your true value. It is important therefore that we understand God's perspectives.

> *"You have not really won until you win in the marketplace"*

WHAT IS VALUE

We are dealing with the subject matter of Commanding Value; but what is value. That is an important question. Webster dictionary defines value as *"...the property or aggregate properties of a thing, that makes it useful or desirable".* The regard that something is held to deserve; the importance or preciousness of something. In other words that **quality or qualities of a thing, which translate it into worth in the mind of somebody else**. Now what does that tell you? It tells you instantly that there are **three dimensions of value**. If you understand these principles; you will begin to see how the rich think. Part of the challenge sometimes is that some of us don't know the mentality of the wealthy and how they think.

The first dimension of value is what I call **Rational Value**. Rational value is (you want to buy a car, you are given a Mercedes on the right hand side, on the left hand side is a Ford Escort. So your instinct tells you that the Mercedes is worth more than the Ford Escort) cerebral or rational values. Things that have value because they make sense for it to be valuable. That is rational value.

The second dimension of value is what I call **Emotional or Irrational Value**. Emotional or Irrational value is when the perception of value of something is linked to a particular or peculiar interest of the person in that particular area. For example why would somebody buy a painting for £50Million – a tiny piece of painting? Or you go somewhere where they sell star wars memorabilia. Or Elvis memorabilia and pay ridiculous amounts for the shirt Elvis wore in 1965 – someone will pay 10 million dollars for it. What has the shirt Elvis wore got to do with anything? The value that person has attached is no longer rational. It is now purely emotional or sentimental. Things we therefore consider valuable not because it makes sense but because we just have peculiar emotional attachment to it. Therefore we give it value based on that emotion.

The third dimension is what I call **Political / Pragmatic or**

Self Interest Value. In other words we give value to things because we think it is politically sensible to do so. I give value to it because it might advance my career. I give value to it because if I do that my boss likes it. I remember in the early 90s I went for a job somewhere in Surrey, England. That was the last stage of the interview I had passed all the other stages. I was to meet the MD and two other directors of the company. As I got there I noticed that they had lots of pictures of England rugby players. I asked if they enjoy rugby. And stupid me, I spent the next ten minutes telling them how useless rugby is. I think it is a violent sports, useless sports and they listened carefully. The next day I did not get the job.

Later on I was practically told by the secretary that the chairman said that "I have never met someone who hates rugby so much. How can I be seeing that kind of person every day?" Now what I simply did was that I rubbished what was valuable to him. So they did not call me to come and discuss rugby but naively I opened my mouth to talk about rugby. I thought that was a way of breaking the ice. I did not know that I was breaking more than the ice. But the point I am trying to make is that some people have some kind of political self-interest attachment to things.

I remember another job interview I went after that one, the chairman doing the interview asked me which football club I supported? And I told him that I don't support any club. I support the winning side. He insisted "you must have a team you support". So I looked at him and wondered which club can a man like this support? Because I knew that if I mention the "wrong" club, or a club that he considers an enemy of his own; I may find myself in difficulty. I didn't know when Arsenal came out from my mouth (then I was living not far from Highbury, the home of Arsenal). So I said Arsenal and he said "ah! right answer". He said if I had mentioned Tottenham, then I would have been shown the door immediately. Not sure if he was serious or not. But the point is this; we are looking into commanding value. There is a dimension of value that makes sense. But there is a dimension of value that does not make sense.

"There is a dimension of value that makes sense. But there is also a dimension of value that does not make sense"

How do you command value when you are dealing with both quantifiable objective and subjective elements? That is where many people in church run into difficulty. So what do we need to do to move things forward? God has given each and every one of us gifts that we need to stir up. And not stirring up these gifts is a real problem. Everything in life was created with potentials. In other words, in every seed, there is a tree; in ever bird a flock...in every fish a school...in every sheep a flock...in every cow a herd...in every boy a man...in every girl a woman...in every nation a generation. Tragedy strikes when a tree dies in a seed, a man in a boy, a woman in a girl, an idea in a mind. For untold millions, visions die unseen, songs die unsung, plans die unexecuted and futures die buried in the past. The problems of our world go unanswered because potential remains buried.

> *"Everything in life was created with potentials. In other words, in every seed, there is a tree; in ever bird a flock...in every fish a school...in every sheep a flock...in every cow a herd...in every boy a man...in every girl a woman...in every nation a generation"*

You need to understand that what you have is what you will translate into what you want to be. And that translation of a thing is the issue. You need to understand the purpose of something. If you don't understand the purpose, abuse is inevitable. So you need to understand the power of Potential. Your Purpose lives within your Potential and your Value is linked to your Purpose. Potential is dormant ability, reserved power, untapped strength, unused success, hidden talents and capped capability. All you can be but have not yet become; all you can do but have not yet done, how far you can reach but have not yet reached, what you can accomplish but have not yet accomplished.

> *"For untold millions, visions die unseen, songs die unsung, plans die unexecuted and futures die buried in the past. The problems of our world go unanswered because potential remains buried"*

Potential is unexposed ability and latent power. Potential demands that you never settle for what you have accomplished. What you have successfully accomplished is no longer potential. Potential is therefore not what you have done, but what you are yet able to do. Wisdom without perceived value is all too common in our world. Because you have the solution to a big problem does not mean you will command value for it if you don't know how to create and command value.

> *"Your Purpose lives within your Potential and your Value is linked to your Purpose. Potential is dormant ability, reserved power, untapped strength, unused success, hidden talents and capped capability"*

*[14] There was a little city with few men in it; and a great king came against it, besieged it, and built great snares around it. [15] Now there was found in it a poor wise man, and he by his wisdom delivered the city. Yet no one remembered that same poor man. [16] Then I said: " Wisdom is better than strength. Nevertheless **the poor man's wisdom is despised,** And his words are not heard.*
Eccl 9:14-15 (NKJV)

What does this tell you instantly about value? Value is not solely on the quality of what you have but about the strength of how people perceive what you have. Because this poor man did not have to prove his wisdom works, he has already shown that his wisdom works. So despite the fact that his wisdom delivered the city, what happened? There was no value attached to it. So because you have a skill does not mean that people will see it as valuable. Because you have knowledge of something does not make people see it as valuable if you don't package it in the language of value. And the language of value differs from place to place.

"Value is not solely on the quality of what you have but about the strength of how people perceive what you have"

Let me give you practical examples because I need you to get this. During one of my trips to Nigeria in 2011, I had a meeting with one of the Commissioners in Lagos State in his office. So I have to go to the state secretariat. I was told that the governor made an order that no car without a special sticker should be allowed into secretariat premises because they were afraid of bomb attacks. Hence all visitors had to drop by the gate and their driver can go and park somewhere else and you will have to walk and that is what I had to do.

> *"Because you have knowledge of something does not make people see it as valuable if you don't package it in the language of value. And the language of value differs from place to place"*

So when I finished with the commissioner, I had to walk back to the gate and called my driver, and it took a while for him to get back to me at the gate. I stood by the gate watching. I noticed a few things while I was waiting. It was so interesting that I had to go and ask the security men that were there. They look at your car and if there is no sticker, they will refuse you entry and then only those with stickers will pass. Three cars passed that did not have the sticker. Not only did they pass but security staff were busy saluting the occupants.

When I looked at the number plate, they were traditional rulers from Lagos villages. One was from Badagry, another one was from Ikorodu and there was a third one I could not remember. Even though they had no sticker on their car as prescribed by the Governor; their number plate had shown that they are Obas (Traditional Rulers), was sufficient for the security men to allow them inside, saluting along the way. So instantly, I asked one of the security guys: "I thought only those with stickers are supposed to go in; these car did not have any sticker". He said that it was Kabiyesi (Obas) that were in each of the cars. I said "so what"; the cars did not have prescribed sticker.

His response was sharp when he said; "I am not going to be the one to stop a Kabiyesi". Then I said; "So Kabiyesi cannot be a security risk?" And we laughed about it. The point is this; for those security men, the Obas or Kabiyesis as they were called were people of high esteem. For him, they are valuable people. Because they represent value to him, he was happy to break protocol to allow them to pass.

Now if you had five PhDs and you have all your certificates in your hands, and had tried to drive inside the gate; do you know that they will turn back your car without any hesitation. Because that day your PhD means absolutely nothing. It represents Zero Value in that situation. So in that society what represents value is not the same as western or other cultures. And this is the difficulty many Nigerians in the diaspora have when they go back home for instance. They go back home trying to throw the weight of their certificate around and people look at them and just laugh at their lack of understanding. Because they think it is all about having western education.

I had a discussion with a friend of mine and we did an experiment in summer of 2011 in Nigeria. When talking about commanding value, I like testing principles. We wrote twenty letters to twenty different government ministries in Nigeria. On one letterhead we made up a fictitious name and put all the academic degrees; MBA, PhD etc. Using the same body of letter not changing the words of the letter we now used another letter head in which we wrote Otunba (Chief) so and so. Do you know of the twenty that we sent with PhD, we got only five replies. Of the twenty we sent with Otunba (Chief), we got nineteen responses.

What does that tell you instantly? You are dealing with a society that places value on certain things more than other things. I hope you are beginning to understand my analysis. So you don't approach a society with an object that does not represent value to them. If you do, it does not matter how valuable it is to you; you are not going to get value response out of it. You have to learn to package your skill and yourself in a language of value.

Going back to scripture, how did Paul capture this principle? Paul said, to the Jew I am a Jew to those without the law; I am as though without the law even though I am under the law of Christ. All I have said in the last few pages is what Paul has summarized in few verses.

> "*To the Jews* I became as a Jew, that I might win Jews; to men under the Law, [I became] as one under the Law, though not myself being under the Law, that I might win those under the Law.
>
> [21] *To those without (outside) law* I became as one without law, not that I am without the law of God and lawless toward Him, but that I am [especially keeping] within and committed to the law of Christ, that I might win those who are without law.
>
> [22] *To the weak (wanting in discernment)* I have become weak (wanting in discernment) that I might win the weak and overscrupulous. I have [in short] become all things to all men, that I might by all means (at all costs and in any and

every way) save some [by winning them to faith in Jesus Christ].

[23] *And I do this for the sake of the good news (the Gospel), in order that I may become **a participator** in it and share in its [blessings along with you].* **1 Corinthians 9:20-23 (Amplified Bible)**

In other words, when I am with the Jews, I do things that are valuable to the Jews in such a way that if you look at me, the Jews around me will be comfortable around me. They will think I am one of them. But when I am with those without the law or those we call the gentiles, again, I behave as though I am one of them.

For those who do not understand, you need to know that there are cultural elements within the Jewish and the gentile culture that are exact opposites of each other. It means that if you look at Apostle Paul on Monday with the Jews – he won't eat what they don't eat, he will wear what they wear. If on Tuesday, you see him with the gentiles he will change all those things. The things that gentiles eat that the Jews don't eat he will now start eating. I hope I am making sense. Why? Because that is what is valuable to the gentiles. He says "I am all things to all men that I may win some'.

The challenge with many believers is that we have one static approach. So it's a take it or leave it; this is who I am. But we don't understand that wisdom means that you might have to adjust and blend where possible to achieve a greater purpose. But we also see that Apostle Paul put the red line there, when he said *"...I am as though without the law...even though I am under the law of Christ"*. That means there are some areas he will not go in the name of blending in. He has some red lines of boundaries that will allow him to keep his Christian witness. But how many of us can blend the way Paul suggest? We need wisdom to direct us in the way we do things because until what you do represent value to somebody else, he will not respond. The fact that it is valuable to you means nothing. They have to perceive that value too.

> *"We need wisdom to direct us in the way we do things because until what you do represent value to somebody else, he will not respond"*

Sadly, the Church has operated so far based on two extremes. What do I mean by that? On one side there are those who believe God has said it, it will happen even if I don't do anything. This camp believes that God has said it, I believe it and that settles it. I can just fold my hand. And such people circulate within the four walls of their church. They don't circulate beyond that. The other extreme are those who think that God helps those who help themselves. So God can wait let me go and do it my own way. Many have lost their Christian testimony as a result of such adventures into the belly of Babylon. So you have two extremes. But the truth is, there is something in the middle.

> *"Many have lost their Christian testimony as a result of such adventures into the belly of Babylon"*

What I mean by that is you don't get to a point where you say that because God has said it you don't do anything. But also you need understand that when you are in the marketplace, you are not there purely because of your skill. You are there for a reason. One of my mentors used to tell me, he said son "if you are going on a journey and you have never encountered the devil, then you are going in the same direction as he is." Because if you are going in opposite directions, one day there would be a clash. And then if there is no clash just know that devil is behind you or in front of you and you are heading in the same direction.

> *"If you are going on a journey and you have never encountered the devil, then*

you are going in the same direction as he is"

"Because if you are going in opposite directions, one day there would be a clash. And then if there is no clash just know that devil is behind you or in front of you and you are heading in the same direction"

If you look at 1Cor; 9: 20 – 23 the amplified version quoted Apostle Paul saying from verse 23 *"And I do these for the sake of the good news (gospel) in order that I may become a participator in it and share in its blessing with you."* The word "participator" implies that you cannot participate in something without dressing yourself in the language of value to that thing. In other words if I am with the Jews, I choose to participate in what they do. If I am with those without the law, I choose to participate in what they do. Otherwise you become an outsider. People don't respond to outsiders; They respond to people they feel are one of them. We need therefore to understand what the response of the church should be to activities in the Marketplace.

In Acts 17: 16 – 17; there is something Paul discovered when he went to Athens. The Bible says that when he got to the city, Apostle Paul found out that the city was given up to Idolatry. For most of us if we enter a city that is given up to idolatry, we are going to declare a thirty day fast. But what was Apostle Paul's response?

> *"People don't respond to outsiders; They respond to people they feel are one of them. We need therefore to understand what the response of the church should be to activities in the Marketplace"*

> *"Now while Paul waited for them at Athens, his spirit was stirred in him, when he saw the city wholly given to idolatry.[17] Therefore disputed he in the synagogue with the Jews, and with the devout persons, and **in the market daily** with them that met with him".*
>
> Acts 17: 16 – 17 (KJV)

> *"While Paul was waiting for them in Athens, he was deeply troubled by all the idols he saw everywhere in the city. [17] He went to the **synagogue** to reason with the Jews and the God-fearing Gentiles, **and he spoke daily in the public square** to all who happened to be there."*
>
> (NLT)

The Bible says he reasoned with the people in the synagogue (or the church) to address the problem. But for most of us that is all we would have done. But Paul realized that for this to be solved he must address it not only in the synagogue, but he must go beyond. In the same verse the bible says *"therefore he reasoned in the synagogue with the Jews and the gentile worshipers and in the marketplace daily"*. Why? Because he realized that the marketplace is the real battleground.

When you are dealing with something like that in the temple, most of the people are probably not in the temple. So they are not hearing you. You say God has sent me to this city ok but all you do is talk in the church. But as God sent you to this city, if it is this city, then you need to do a lot of work both in the church and outside the church. And that is what Paul was doing here; he addressed it in the church first. But he realized that most of the people in the church are probably not the ones doing the idolatry. So he has to go to where they are and then speak as well.

CHAPTER 3

Biblical Examples of Value Perception And Presentation

APOSTLE PAUL COMMANDED VALUE

I want to present a couple of cases to you to aid your understanding of how to command value. I want to show you in scripture; how Apostle Paul's change of his value perception was necessary before he was able to reach the nations.

In **Acts 13:2-3**; The Bible says:

> ...*The Holy Spirit said, "Set apart for Me Barnabas and Saul..." They...laid hands on them, and sent them away.*

And in **Acts 19:10** ; the Bible then stated:

*...So that ALL who lived in Asia heard the word
of the Lord,*

So they were commissioned in Acts chapter thirteen and
by chapter nineteen, the whole of Asia have heard the
gospel. What I want to bring to your attention here is what
happened between chapters thirteen and nineteen of the
book of Acts. I want to use this to illustrate the reality of
value proposition and how we as believers must be able to
command value.

Let us look at how this started. When Paul started his
ministry in Acts chapter 13 after he was called, he was
perceived purely as a minister or a pastor. I am using the
word pastor here not to limit Apostle Paul's office but to
make it easier for you to understand the fundamentals of
my analysis being between the marketplace and ministry.
So Paul was seen purely as a minister, (as a pastor for want
of a better word or as a priest) in Acts chapter thirteen. But
from Acts chapter 13 to chapter 18 Paul was struggling
with his outreach programmes. He was under immense
attacks which led to several practical impediments in
ministry. Everywhere he went, he was encountering
difficulty. But something happened in **Acts 18** when he
met Aquila and Pricilla.

Paul was a minister of the gospel and Aquila and Pricilla

were successful and influential business people; what we can call the Richard Branson, Dangote or Donald Trumps of this world. They were business couple who knew all the movers and shakers of the cities. Paul went into business partnership with them. Over a short period of time; What happened was that there was an exchange. Paul a minister embraced marketplace work; Aquila and Pricilla who were marketplace professionals equally embraced ministry work.

With this context in mind; we now need to see how Paul used his business value perception and proposition to take the presence and power of God to the marketplace and transform the whole of the region. Let us look at some of the things that happened. I will divide my analysis into **Part 1** and **Part 2**. Part 1 will be Paul's ministry before he met Aquila and Priscilla and Part 2 will be after he went into business with them and through them got to know all the political and economic movers and shakers of the cities.

PART 1 – *Apostle Paul's value perception was purely as a Pastor / Minister only*

i).   Location: PISIDIAN ANTIOCH in ACTS 13.

WHAT HAPPENED IN THE CITY?

> *v. 44, 49 - ...Nearly the whole city assembled to hear the word of God...And the word of the Lord was being spread through the whole region.*

WHAT WAS THE REACTION?

> *v. 50 ...The devout women of prominence and the leading men of the city...instigated a persecution against Paul and Barnabas...*

THE RESULT?

> *v. 10 ...(They) drove them (Paul & his Team) out of their district.*

ii).   Location: THESSALONICA in ACTS 17.

WHAT HAPPENED IN THE CITY?

> *v. 4 ...Were persuaded and joined Paul and Silas, along with a great multitude of the God-fearing Greeks and a number of the leading women.*

WHAT WAS THE REACTION?

> *v.5 ...wicked men from the marketplace, formed a mob and set the city in an uproar...*
> *v.8 ...And they stirred up the crowd and the city authorities.*

THE RESULT?

> *v.10 ...And [they] sent Paul and Silas away by night*

So after these experiences, Paul met Aquila and Priscilla and went into business partnership with them from Acts 18. Consequently, Paul began to interact with all the top political, judicial and business figures in the cities; not as a Minister of the gospel but as a Businessman in the Marketplace who happens to be a Minister as well. So gradually Paul's value perception began to change from purely religious to that of a successful businessman who is contributing to the wealth of the cities; thus deserving political patronage. Now let us examine what happened to the ministry of Apostle Paul due to the changed value perception.

PART 2 – *Apostle Paul's value perception was now predominantly as a Businessman in the Marketplace who* *happens to be a minister of the gospel as well.*

i).   Location: CORINTH in ACTS 18.
WHAT HAPPENED IN THE CITY?

> *v.8 - ....And many of the Corinthians when they heard were believing and being baptized....*

WHAT WAS THE REACTION?

> *v.12 ...the Jews with one accord rose up against Paul and brought him before the judgment*

THE RESULT?

> *v.14, 16 ...(The proconsul) drove (the Jews) away from the judgment seat.*
> *v.18 - And Paul...remained many days longer....*

ii).   Location: EPHESUS in ACTS 19.

WHAT HAPPENED IN THE CITY?

> *v.20 - The word of the Lord was growing mightily and prevailing.*

WHAT WAS THE REACTION?

> *v.23 ... There arose no small disturbance...*
> *v.29 ... The city was filled with the confusion,*
> *and they rushed...into the theater.*

THE RESULT?

> *v.31 - ...Some of the Asiarchs who were friends*
> *of (Paul) ...urged him not to venture into the*
> *theater.*
> *v.35,41 - ...After quieting the multitude.....the*
> *town clerk...dismissed the assembly.*

So we can see from the above analysis that Paul had a better outcome for the gospel after his public perception changed from Part 1 to Part 2. As his influence in the marketplace increases; Paul's ministry advanced more. So instead of being whisked away at night in part 1, he remained many days after in part 2. So the setbacks he experienced in Antioch and Thessalonica were replaced with victories in Corinth and Ephesus. What changed was Paul Value Perception in the Marketplace.

After Paul became business partners with Aquila and Pricilla, he must have attended several business meetings; thus Paul became friends with the city clerks, the mayors with all the political powers of the city, because Aquila and Pricilla knew all these people. That is why for instance in Acts 18; the Proconsul, who is now a chum of Paul, drove the Jews out. And you begin to see the difference in the outcome for his ministry. You notice that in both Part 1 and Part 2, the reaction of the people remained constant. But to the powers that be, Paul was no longer a stranger to them. That became a significant leverage for Paul.

We now begin to see how gospel begin to spread through the whole of Asia in Acts nineteen. The journey to it was achieved by Paul embracing the marketplace, increasing his value proposition in the marketplace and willing to understand that we must not isolate ourselves as a church otherwise our ability to function in our cities would be impossible. So people raised up objections against Apostle Paul but when they got to the people who would make the judgment they said "Oh its Paul, don't worry. No case to answer!" They drove the people away from the judgment seat.

> *"The journey to it was achieved by Paul embracing the marketplace, increasing his value proposition in the marketplace and willing to understand that we must not isolate ourselves as a church*

*otherwise our ability to function in our
cities would be impossible"*

And what happened after that? Rather than being driven
out by night, Paul now remained there many days longer.
In other words there is no running away anymore. Why?
Because he was no longer just a minister, now he knew
people in the marketplace and he was now speaking the
language of value to the people in the marketplace. One
thing you will notice here is that the anointing of Apostle
Paul in Antioch and Thessalonica is the same as the
anointing on him in Ephesus and Corinth. So his
anointing has not increased or decreased. This mean that
this is not about spiritual anointing per se; the only
difference is that he is now known to the powers that be.
Through his involvement in the marketplace; Paul now
represented value to them. And we can see how that
instantly impacts the spread of the gospel. So instead of
him running away overnight and couldn't preach, he now
stayed many days longer preaching heavily. So the gospel
is now securing inroad because we have value in the
marketplace.

For example in the UK; many churches complain of
difficulty in getting Planning Permission to build or
convert premises to churches. In many cases; the reason
for the difficulty is that many churches offer purely

religious value proposition with little or no impact in the marketplace (communities). We need to understand that there is a language we can speak that will compel positive outcomes for these planning applications. That is why so many times, Satan is astonished at the kind of accusations levelled against him by Christians. Because we blame him for things he himself does not know anything about. It is the way we have packaged ourselves that has limited our manifestations in many areas. So this is the first biblical example of how change in value proposition can advance the gospel of the Kingdom.

> *"Satan is astonished at the kind of accusations levelled against him by Christians. Because we blame him for things he himself does not know anything about"*

JOSEPH COMMANDED VALUE

I want us to also examine a second biblical case study. It is the case of Joseph. When he was called to the palace; Joseph endeavoured to present himself in a way that projected value to Pharaoh. Despite his ability to interpret dreams; he knew he will not last in front of the king if he did not present himself in a way that will be acceptable to the king.

> *"Then Pharaoh **sent and called Joseph**, and they brought him quickly out of the dungeon; and **he (Joseph) SHAVED, CHANGED his CLOTHING**, and came to Pharaoh." - **Genesis 41:14** (NKJV*

Why did Joseph have to change his appearance? Why could he not just rely on his anointing alone? Why did he have to present himself in a way that speaks value to the king? These are essential questions indeed. The Egyptian aristocracy who had access to Pharaoh, were known to be completely shaven, they had no body hair at all. And even Pharaoh in those days, his hair is shaven his beard was shaven but they put artificial beard on and occasionally put on hats because of the heat.

JOSEPH was Anointed & Gifted by God; yet needed to speak the Language of Value before Pharaoh. WHY!!!

- In early Egypt; men unshaven later became known as "**barbarians**" meaning the "**unbarbered**".
- The Egyptians had an almost unhealthy personal obsession with body hygiene - and curious customs to accompany it. Priests believed that body hair was shameful and unclean.

- The Greek historian Herodotus (485-425BC) commented that the **Egyptians bathed several times a day** and **"set cleanliness above seemliness"**.
- Egyptian men thought that wearing facial hair was a sign of personal neglect. Being Shaven was seen as being part of the Noble class.

So it may not have pleased the king to see that he was receiving wisdom from a peasant slave. So Joseph had to present himself in a way that speaks value to the king.

So if you are not shaven; The moment you are sighted, they may not even take you to Pharaoh, because your value perception drops. So when Joseph was eventually called out of prison to come to Pharaoh's palace, Joseph's anointing was not in doubt. His ability to interpret dreams was not in doubt. The gift God has given him was beyond doubt. But Joseph thought of something and said "for me to able to win here, I need to dress and portray myself in a language of value". What did he do? He shaved all his hair. This guy was anointed. The Bible says that he was prosperous in prison because the Lord was with him. Spiritually there was no issue here. But he understood that he was going to Pharaoh's palace and he needed to present himself in a way Pharaoh will not say "who is this man? Get him out!"

He may not even be in the king's presence long enough to interpret the dream. If he did not have the appearance that is consistent with the value Pharaoh places on his advisers. Hence he instantly decided to shave. Personally; as far as Joseph was concerned whether he had facial hairs or not made no difference to him. But it made a difference to his intended audience. He shaved and he changed his clothing. Why? Because he was dressing for where he was going; not where he was coming from. And many of us in life, we are dressing for where we are coming from. Our dressing reveals to people where we are coming from. But your dressing should reveal where you are going.

It is important that if you are going for a job interview and you are leaving your house, you don't dress as if you are coming from home; but you dress as if you are going into an office. You dress as if you are going for an interview. So your destination should always inform you value presentation. That is what Joseph did here in Genesis 41.

> *"Our dressing reveals to people where we are coming from. But your dressing should reveal where you are going"*

Joseph's gifting and anointing may not have been received and allowed to manifest if he did not speak the Egyptian Value Language. Lack of understanding of the Language of Value, could hinder opportunities to demonstrate your Anointing & Gifting.

We are looking at the subject matter commanding value; and in the stories of Paul and Joseph we have seen the biblical examples for us to package our gift in a language of value if we are to receive the right reception in the marketplace and become participators in matters of global economics. The anointing on these men is not in question here. Without a doubt they were both anointed. But we understand that the perception of the value they represented was not a function of their anointing; it was a function of how they engaged with the marketplace. It was a question of how they packaged their gifts in the language of value. This is a key principle of kingdom advancement.

Therefore while this principle could have some benefit for interpersonal relationships within the church; that is not the salient consideration. This principle is not supposed to dominate the relationship between a Pastor and his congregation for instance. But; it is the main factor that will govern the relationships between the Church and the Marketplace; between the Pastor and the communities in which the church is located, between the believer and the unbeliever, between the spiritual and the secular. We must speak in the language of our audience and not in our own if we are to communicate.

> *"We must speak in the language of our audience and not in our own if we are to communicate"*

CHAPTER 4

The Containers of Value

So, what are the carriers of value. What are the things that represent value to people out there? Truth is, the Church has been shooting herself in the foot in the way we have been conducting ourselves in ways that do not portray value to our audience. For example one of the things that is a problem in the church is a sense in most people's mind that when it comes to church, everything should be free. There is this sense of entitlement that we have. We are happy to pay for something outside the church; but the moment the same is offered by the Church; many immediately expect it to be free.

This is best illustrated by the story of a believer that attends a church in south London. He observed that there was increasing number of unemployed and underemployed folks in the church; so he decided he would try and help them. He decided to use his own skill to train them in Prince2 Project Management Methodology, so that at the end of the one-week training they will sit for the Prince2 exam to get certified as Project Managers. This brother had to hire a meeting room in a hotel near the church for the training.

To cover the cost of the meeting room only he decided to charge £70 per participant for the whole week's training that will lead to Prince2 certification; but he will offer his expertise for free. This guy could not believe his ears when majority of folks in the church complained to the Pastor that the brother was charging too much and he should have done the whole thing for free; that after all it is a "Church" thing. As a result many people in the church did not come because there was a token charge for the training. Now a basic research will reveal that the cheapest Prince2 Project Management Certification training available in London was £1100. Yet in church seventy quid was too expensive for most. This story reveals the reason why poverty is entrenched in our churches. People don't invest in themselves. Many of the people that complained about the £70 charge in the church could easily afford the money; they just didn't believe that any specialised programme being offered from within the church should be chargeable. They think it is all about prayer and fasting. Consequently; the container of value in most of Christendom is Price.

Price of something becomes the determinant of its value to many believers. But price is the lowest container of value; yet that is the emphasis of most church folk. In fact, in economics, there are some products or goods called Giffen goods. In economics and consumer theory, a Giffen good is one which people paradoxically consume more of as the price rises, violating the law of demand. That is; a consumer good for which demand rises when the price increases, and demand falls when the price decreases. In other words the normal law of economics says that the lower the price the higher the demand. But Giffen goods work the other way round. The high the price; the higher the demand. So Price is not the best predictor of value. Cheap may be more expensive in the long run. The Church need to develop better understanding of the value concept.

"Price is the lowest container of value; yet that is the emphasis of most church folk"

An example is diamond. If someone brings a coin-sized diamond to you and says this is forty quid what are you going to say? Most people will turn it down. So the lower the price, the less the demand. Whereas if you are given diamond and asked to pay ten thousand pounds you go ahead and give him the money. If you don't have the money, you will say let me save for the diamond. So the higher the price, the higher the value perception. That shows you that price is nothing always a reliable communicator of value. But sadly to most in the Church price has become the major container of value. To the extent that if churches have specialized developmental event (such as Couples Dinner etc); and folks are told to pay twenty quid for instance; you will see that many people won't come. The same person will eat four McDonalds meals that week. Many cannot get pass the fact that everything coming from the church MUST BE FREE. Price has become the main value container for most church folks. Sadly; this worldview is exactly what keeps people poor in perpetuity.

> *"Cheap may be more expensive in the long run. The Church need to develop better understanding of the value concept"*

This is why many are not making progress as they should. Because they are not investing in themselves. The problems this creates for the church is; since most are expecting things to be free, (because price has become a major container of value for us), it now also affects what believers charge for their own services as entrepreneurs. Many times I see a Christian in business and I ask how much is your charge for X? And he says for instance, sixty quid. I scream. This is something that unbelievers and other businesses charge three hundred quid for. I then ask why they don't charge more and the response is always the same: *people won't pay*. My response is usually; no you won't pay. Because you won't pay, you assume nobody else would. *"Cheap calleth to the cheap";* so to speak. Am I making sense?

My oldest daughter went with me early in 2012, to Switzerland. She was in her second year in the university at that time. She got an email while there from a company asking her to blog for them for an event. She is a blogger amongst other things. They offered to pay her two hundred quid for the day. So she was telling me that they wanted her to confirm her acceptance that day. I asked her the name of the company and she mentioned it. I told her they were offering her very low rate (although she was excited to be getting £200 extra income).

I insisted that she should charge based on a better value of her services and encouraged her to respond in a particular way that goes like: *"… normally I charge five hundred pounds for such services, but to kick start a mutually beneficial relationship I am happy to discount the charge to four hundred and fifty pounds on this occasion…."*. My daughter screamed and was concerned the company won't pay. She said what if they say no. I assured her that if they say no, she has not lost anything; but would have maintained her value. She sent the email and they responded within an hour to say four hundred and fifty pounds is ok for them and thanking her for the discount. She was ecstatic. I simply showed her how to present her gift in a language of value. You need to understand that life does not give you what you deserve; it gives you what you negotiate. And never negotiate from a position of weakness.

There is a principle in economics which says something like this: *"if every means of production is given the value of its commensurate output, the company will go burst"*. In other words, if a company employs ten people, and assuming those ten people are all the means of production, and that every month the company makes a £1000 in profit. Which means the average value of each person's output is £100. If the company pays each staff £100 (the true value of their output); What is going to happen to the company? It will fold up because there is no profit. This means capitalism demands that you can never be paid the value of your output. Because if you are paid the value of your output, your employer will be out of business.

> *"You need to understand that life does not give you what you deserve; it gives you what you negotiate. And never negotiate from a position of weakness"*

So the basis of capitalism is exploitation which creates a situation where the value of your output is £100; but you will be paid £10 as salary. And then the employer pockets the remaining £90. Even the companies that you say are paying better, they might pay £20 out of the £100; hence they are better than the one that paid £10. But NOBODY (as an employee) is ever paid the true value of their output, because if they do, the employer will be out of business. What does that tell you? That when you are working in the marketplace, you can never be paid the true value of your output. Hence, the value you represent to the employer will determine how much of your output you will be paid.

But then God steps in to bridge the gap for His saints. He brought his own economic law – the Law of Reward. This law states that: *"…a labourer is worthy of his hire", (Luke 10:7).* This scripture has several meaning. But a dimension of it can be said to be God saying to the employee; *don't worry, if you work for anybody, I know that they will never pay you the value of your labour. But as long as you perform your job as unto the Lord; giving your best, I (God) will make it up to you supernaturally.* Therefore for whatever they don't pay you, I will make it up. Because God has a way of making sure that a labourer must be rewarded for his hire. The law of reward is used to compensate you for the failings of the law of economics that says you can never be paid for the value of your output, Praise God.

*"The value you represent to the employer
will determine how much of your output
you will be paid"*

Sometimes the issue for many of us is not whether we are
anointed, but whether we can package what we have been
given in a language that portrays value. Joseph's gifts and
anointing could not have been received or allowed to
manifest if he did not dress himself in a language of value.
And that is the problem with the many folks in today's
church.

*"The law of reward is used to compensate
you for the failings of the law of
economics that says you can never be
paid for the value of your output"*

Apostle Paul said that he became all things to all men that
he might win some. We need to appreciate the fact that
what represents value in the church is not the same thing as
outside the church. Many people are not just in church but
they are locked up in it; to the extent that they speak only
church language. We need to change our outlook when we
are in the marketplace to best present ourselves in a way
that command value. You have to learn how to switch in
the marketplace. This is what helped Apostle Paul, he

learnt to switch away from church mind-set in the marketplace.

The problem with many believers is that we do not know how to switch and we go on and apply the same "Church approach to business and fail every time. Paul was able to switch to suit his intended audience. This is the skill lacking in the church today. Many believers do not know how to switch. They approach the Marketplace with the same emotional framework as in the Church. Hence the high failure rate of Christian businesses the world over. The Language of Value in the Church is different from that in the Marketplace. So if you do not switch you will be speaking Greek to an Hebrew speaker. There will be no communication with your intended audience. Worse still, many of your words could mean the opposite to your audience, thus causing offence and failure.

> *"The Language of Value in the Church is different from that in the Marketplace. So if you do not switch you will be speaking Greek to an Hebrew speaker"*

CONTAINERS OF CORPORATE VALUE

If you manage a business, what are the measurements of

corporate value? What are the things that make your business valuable? What are the containers or vehicles your value is embedded in? Here are some for you to consider.

1.   QUALITY: The quality of your product is a significant container of value. People will pay more for quality if proven. For example, take Apple computers. People pay more for this brand of computers, because of its proven quality. With the cost of one apple computer, you can buy three other PC based computers. But people who buy apple know that they are paying for quality. Therefore quality can attract value.

2.   CONVENIENCE: Another thing that command value business-wise is convenience. That is why for example many of the high street shops are suffering (in many Western countries) because of the proliferation of large convenient Malls, Superstores and Shopping centers. The idea of going to one place and being able to buy everything under one roof is very powerful and appealing. A lot of people find that convenient, rather than going to shop 1 and buying one thing and shop 2 to buy another one and they are tired walking down a high street. They rather go to one place and do everything. Convenience attracts value.

3. **PRICE:** Price is also a determinant of value clearly for some items. Some people buy some things purely because of price. But as I have already explained; price is not always a strong indication of value.

4. **TRUST:** This is where the key issue is. It does not matter what your price is; if people do not trust you, they won't buy your products. So trust is very fundamental. Trust is very important.

5. **IMAGE:** In measurement of corporate value, your image matters. Your image will determine whether people want to be seen in your product or not. If your image is a reigning image, people will rush to buy your product. One thing I don't do regardless of your image is that I will never advertise you without you paying for it. So you will never see me in any T-shirt with any brand written on it, say Armani. Why would I advertise for free? Image for some people is a function of their wanting to look cool; hence they are willing to pay a premium for it.

6. **TIME OR SPEED:** People pay more for something that is quicker. That is why you pay more for first class than second postage. And if you want it as guaranteed next day delivery, that even cost more. People still pay for that because speed is important to most of us.

7.   **SAFETY:** People will pay for something that is safer, especially products that relates to kids. People will pay premium for something that is safe than for something that is cheap and could cause some manner of problem.

So for your business to command value; you need to pay attention to these things; all of them, not just the Price only.

CONTAINERS OF PERSONAL VALUE

Now what are the containers of value for you as an employee? For you who are working in an organization, what are some of the key vehicles of your value?

1.   **QUALITY OF YOUR OUTPUT:** If you give your boss back a completed task and he realizes that everybody else do not perform to the same high standard; but when he gives you, it is as good as finished, that quality begins to speak the language of value. You begin to distinguish yourself from the rest. That makes you an asset to the organization.

2.   **SKILL:** Skill including speed of work. If you come to a place and you start doing in three day what others have been taking three week to do, instantly you portray your value. You command value instantly.

3.   **COST TO THE BUSINESS:** Your cost to the business is always a product of your direct cost and revenue generated (or savings made). In other words, how much are they paying you and how much are you generating for them. The lower your net cost to the business, the more valuable you are. Even if they are paying you more but you make them much more money for them, you are still considered valuable. For instance, the highest paid people in the bank are the ones that make the highest money, so the bank still considers them valuable. They are paid more than the rest of the people, because they make more money for the organization.

How do you fit into the strategy of where the business is going? You have a job, you are doing very well, but you don't like computers. Meanwhile the new strategy of the business is to make everything electronic. Instantly, you have lost a job for yourself, because your position is inconsistent with the current strategy of the company you are working for. It is important for you to understand that fitting into the future strategic direction of the firm is key.

4.   **RELIABILITY AND COMMITMENT:** That includes time keeping. How reliable are you? Is your word worth anything? Do you keep to deadlines? These are elements that allow you to command value personally. You will also become a force for good in your organization

by influencing other people for good.

5.   RELATIONAL AND TEAM DYNAMICS: In other words how do you work well with the other team members. If you are the most skilled person, but you are always fighting with your other colleagues, you will not last. It is important that you look at your impact on the team as a whole. You may be the number one when it comes to skill and knowledge, but if you are always the one everybody complains about, you won't last. So you need to be able to work as part of a team. It is important because your employer knows that he cannot run that department with you alone.

6.   DIVINE FAVOUR: It is very important that you do not rule out divine favour. Favour has the capability to distinguish you and make you established in whatever you do. It is impossible to bye-pass God's favour and make it to the top. Divine favour dimension is very crucial for your lifting and ability to command personal value. When He decides to promote you, no personalities or principalities can bring you down again! There are many benefits that will accrue to a man that is favoured. Amongst which is to break protocols and natural rules to give undue kindness to an individual. Esther was a queen in a foreign Land, Mary conceived a child without meeting a man. All these people are recipients of Divine favour, and certain rules were broken for them to enjoy exceptional privileges. This can be your testimony too. Amen!

> *"When He decides to promote you, no personalities or principalities can bring you down again"*

CHAPTER 5

The Place of Purpose
In Commanding Value

To be able to command value, you must be able to first understand your purpose. Because the value of zero is still zero; the value of nothing is nothing. If you don't understand your purpose in life, it is going to be difficult for you to command value. Why? Because commanding value is not an artificial thing; it is about your passion. What do I mean by that? There is a difference between your work and you job.

Your job is what you are paid to do. Your work is what you are born to do. You need to understand that the only way you begin to work in kingdom abundance, as you should is when your work and job combines into one. What do I mean? The bible says in Ecclesiastes 11:6; *"In the morning sow thy seed, and in the evening withhold not thine hand: for thou knowest not whether shall prosper, either this or that, or whether they both shall be alike good".*

What does that mean? In the day do your job, in the evening do not withhold your hand, do your work. If your work and your job are not the same thing; you need to work your work to become your job. What do this mean? Your job is what you are paid to do; your work is what you are born to do.

I am linking this to purpose; that is, you coming to an understanding of your purpose. What is it that if you are woken up by 2 am in the morning to do you will do gladly? That is beginning to give you an idea of what purpose is. And once you understand that, your work should be in that same area. Some of you are doing jobs that do not reflect your work. And that is why you are constantly afraid of redundancy. You can be sacked from your job, but you can never be sacked from your work. When you are doing your work, you are unsackable because you are using what is your God given gift, your purpose in life. Yes in the day you will do some job to put food on the table to start with; but in the evening begin to work towards discovering your purpose and working your purpose out.

> *But Jesus answered them, My Father worketh hitherto, and I work.*
>
> - John 5:17

Jesus did not say I have a job, he said *"my father worketh heretheto I work"*. There is a difference between your work and your job. How do you now discover your purpose which gives birth to your work? Some of the questions you have to ask are what are your core competences? What are the things you love doing? What do you do in your free time? What do you notice you do repeatedly and habitually?

> *"Your job is what you are paid to do; your work is what you are born to do"*

What are those things that spark your creativity? What do people complement you on? What would you do if you know you could not fail? The important thing I am saying about all those things is that you need to discover your purpose first. Then you wrap your value around your purpose. You cannot have value without a purpose, because the value of nothing is nothing. Your value is an effective representation of your purpose. It is important for you to understand this.

> *"You can be sacked from your job, but you can never be sacked from your work"*

WHAT IS YOUR GIFT?

"AS FOR myself, brethren, when I came to you, I did not come proclaiming to you the testimony and evidence or ¹1¹ mystery and secret of God [concerning what He has done through Christ for the salvation of men] in lofty words of eloquence or human philosophy and wisdom; ²For I resolved to know nothing (to be acquainted with nothing, to make a display of the knowledge of nothing, and to be conscious of nothing) among you except Jesus Christ (the Messiah) and Him crucified. ³And I was in passed into a state of) weakness and fear (dread) and great trembling after I had come] among you. ⁴And my language and my message were not set forth in persuasive (enticing and plausible) words of wisdom, but they were in demonstration of the [Holy] Spirit and power a proof by the Spirit and power of God, operating on me and stirring in the minds of my hearers the most holy emotions and thus persuading them], ⁵So that your faith might not rest in the wisdom of men (human philosophy), but in the power of God".

1 Corinthians 2:1-5 (AMP)

"So too the [Holy] Spirit comes to our aid and bears us up in our weakness; for we do not know what prayer to offer nor how to offer it worthily as we ought, but the Spirit Himself goes to meet our supplication and pleads in our behalf with unspeakable yearnings and groanings too deep for utterance".

Romans 8:26 (NKJV)

Weakness can be described as the inability to produce result. If you learn to yield your weaknesses to God then you will get to a place where His grace will abound towards you. You will banish your inability to produce result today in Jesus Name. Amen!

*"For the kingdom of heaven is like a man travelling to a far country, who called his own servants and delivered his goods to them. [15] And to one he gave five talents, to another two, and to another one, **to each according to his own ability**; and immediately he went on a journey. [16] Then he who had received the five talents went and traded with them, and made another five talents. [17] And likewise he who had received two gained two more also. [18] But he who had received one went and dug in the ground, and hid his lord's money. [19] After a long time the lord of those*

servants came and settled accounts with them.
[20] "So he who had received five talents came and brought five other talents, saying, "Lord, you delivered to me five talents; look, I have gained five more talents besides them.' [21] His lord said to him, "Well done, good and faithful servant; you were faithful over a few things, I will make you ruler over many things. Enter into the joy of your lord.'……

[24] "Then he who had received the one talent came and said, "Lord, I knew you to be a hard man, reaping where you have not sown, and gathering where you have not scattered seed. [25] And I was afraid, and went and hid your talent in the ground. Look, there you have what is yours.' [26] "But his lord answered and said to him, "You wicked and lazy servant, you knew that I reap where I have not sown, and gather where I have not scattered seed. [27] So you ought to have deposited my money with the bankers, and at my coming I would have received back my own with interest. [28] So take the talent from him, and give it to him who has ten talents. [29] "For to everyone **who has, more will be given,** *and he will have abundance; but from him who does not have,*

even what he has will be taken away. [30] And cast the unprofitable servant into the outer darkness. There will be weeping and gnashing of teeth.'
- Matthew 25:14-30

God has given all of us talents. But why are people not able to produce result like this wicked servant? Each time there is an inability to produce in your life, it is because you have not identified, or invested your God given talents; which is your Work. Each time there is an inability to produce in your life; it is because you have invested your time in areas where you have no talents.

"You need to discover your purpose first. Then you wrap your value around your purpose. You cannot have value without a purpose, because the value of nothing is nothing"

So you need to know, What is your ability, and How you can enjoy perpetual increase. This will enable you to then command value. Everything you need has already been given to you by God. All you need is to produce and increase. *I can do all things.......... Through Christ who strengthens me.* But God's strength is only available in the area of your God-given talents and abilities.

"Each time there is an inability to produce in your life, it is because you have not identified, or invested your God given talents; which is your Work"

HOW DO YOU KNOW WHAT YOUR PRIMARY GIFTS ARE?

7 Categories of Christian Talents or Enterprise that results in Increase

[1]*Now concerning spiritual gifts, brethren, I do not want you to be ignorant:* [2]*You know that you were Gentiles, carried away to these dumb idols, however you were led.* [3]*Therefore I make known to you that no one speaking by the Spirit of God calls Jesus accursed, and no one can say that Jesus is Lord except by the Holy Spirit.* [4]*There are diversities of gifts, but the same Spirit.* [5]*There are differences of ministries, but the same Lord.* [6]*And there are diversities of activities, but it is the same God who works all in all.* [7]***But the manifestation of the Spirit is given to each one for the profit of all:*** [8]*for to one is given the word of wisdom through the Spirit, to another the word of knowledge through the same Spirit,* [9]*to another faith by the same Spirit, to another gifts of*

healings by the same|2| Spirit, [10]to another the working of miracles, to another prophecy, to another discerning of spirits, to another different kinds of tongues, to another the interpretation of tongues. [11]But one and the **same Spirit works** all these things, distributing to each one individually as He wills. [12] For as the **body** is one and has many members, but all the members of that one body, being many, are one body, so also is Christ. [13]For by one Spirit we were all baptized into one body--whether Jews or Greeks, whether slaves or free--and have all been made to drink into|3| one Spirit. [14]For in fact the body is not one member but many. [15]If the **foot** should say, "Because I am not a **hand**, I am not of the body," is it therefore not of the body? [16]And if the **ear** should say, "Because I am not an **eye**, I am not of the body," is it therefore not of the body? [17]If the whole body were an eye, where would be the hearing? If the whole were hearing, where would be the **smelling (NOSE)**? [18]But now **God has set the members, each one of them, in the body just as He pleased**. [19]And if they were all one member, where would the body be? [20]But now indeed there are many members (TALENTS), yet one body (MISSION). [21]And the eye cannot

*say to the hand, "I have no need of you"; nor
again the head to the feet, "I have no need of you.*

1 Corinthians 12:1-21

Foot cannot do the work of hand. Eyes cannot do the work
of eye. But which part are you.

> *"Idols make it impossible for a believer to
> command value. Anything that you have
> elevated above God in your life is an idol"*

*[1]Not unto us, O LORD, not unto us, But to Your
name give glory, Because of Your mercy,
Because of Your truth. [2]Why should the Gentiles
say, "So where is their God?" [3]But our God is in
heaven; He does whatever He pleases. [4]**Their
idols are silver and gold,** The work of men's
hands. [5]They have **mouths,** but they do not
speak; **Eyes** they have, but they do not see; [6]They
have **ears,** but they do not hear; **Noses** they have,
but they do not smell; [7]They have **hands,** but they
do not handle; **Feet** they have, but they do not
walk; Nor do they mutter through their throat.
[8]Those who make them are like them; So is
everyone who trusts in them.*

Psalm 115:1-8

IDOLS Makes your talents useless and unfruitful. Because:

- The Eyes of the idol cannot see
- The nose of the idol cannot smell
- The feet of the Idol cannot walk
- The hands of the idol cannot handle
- The ears of the idol cannot hear

Until you get rid of idols in your life your talents (Gifts) cannot come alive. Idols make it impossible for a believer to command value. Anything that you have elevated above God in your life is an idol. It can be money, your assets, your career, your spouse or even your ministry. Therefore, there are six types of People in the Kingdom of God. You need to locate yourself before you can experience effective Increase.

Hand, Feet, Ear, Eye, Nose, Mouth; which are you?

GROUPS OR TYPE OF CHRISTIAN ENTERPRISE OR GIFTEDNESS.

TALENT 1. Hand Group

These are **Artisans, Handcraft, Sculptures, Painters, Hairdressers, Artists**; they can create anything with their hands.

Many of them in the Bible are artisans. Hand type people may not necessarily be academically brilliant. They make money out of their hands creativity. Forcing people like that to go and get degrees upon degrees may be useless.

1 Corinthians 4 - [12]*And we labour, working with our own hands. Being reviled, we bless; being persecuted, we endure;* [13]*being defamed, we entreat. We have been made as the filth of the world, the offscouring of all things until now.*

TALENT 2. FEET Group
The feet people are usually **pioneers and innovators**. They are foot soldiers.

They cannot stay at home. They cannot stay behind a desk. If they do they will become frustrated. They are mobile people. They are outdoor people. If you are the foot type, stop wasting your time applying for jobs you can't get. Why have you stayed unemployed for months and years, believing God, when you could have been making money using your hands? Learn to understand that if we are all office managers who will fix your drains when it is faulty. Stay in the area of your giftedness.

TALENT 3. EAR Group
These are speculators. They pick up things from God's transmitter. They are Investors. Brokers, Stock market

workers. They are prophetic in their hearing. They usually have their ears to the ground. They know what is going to move before anyone else. They could hear money making tips from what others ignore.

TALENT 4. EYE Group

The eye people are visionaries. They make something out of nothing. They are dreamers. Their strength is in their ability to foresee. They see things and capitalise on them. They are leaders who inspire others. They make money out of motivating others in a set direction. *(eg Bill Gates)* They see potentials where others see junk.

TALENT 5. NOSE Group

These are wheeler dealers. They connect. They have connections in high places. This type of people have lots of unbeliever connections. God can use these people to take wealth out of the sinners. They can smell a deal one mile off. They have brief cases, sometime no office. They get contracts and they subcontract to the experts and pocket the profit.

The first chunk of money I made as a business person was in 1989. All I did was to get a contract from an oil company through a contact, then gave it to the real professionals and pocket the difference. So what can you smell?

TALENT 6. MOUTH Group

These are motivational speakers, Orators. They are commentators, Sales people. They are Newscasters. They are Preachers and Teachers. They are lawyers; they are Advocates. These people do a lot of research and study to get their facts right; then they deliver the message with authority. By the way if you are the mouth type, you must take care of your mouth. Smelling mouth is a weapon of mass destruction.

The 7th and final group is the **HEAD group**. This is symbolised by Jesus Himself. He is the one that places you as the eyes, nose, mouth, feet in the body. He is the Head of the Body. He coordinates everything.

But there are people He uses in this capacity as captains. Men like Moses, Solomon, and Nehemiah. They are thinkers. Strategists. They ooze out ideas. They let Jesus influence their mind and thoughts for productivity.

OCCUPY TILL I COME

Luke 19 (NKJV) - *[13] So he called ten of his servants, delivered to them ten minas,[1] and said to them,* **"Do business till I come.'**

...........................*'Put this money to work,'* he said, *'until I come back.'* **(NIV)**

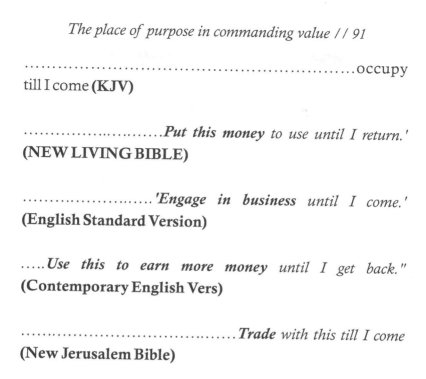

....occupy
till I come **(KJV)**

.........................***Put this money*** *to use until I return.'*
(NEW LIVING BIBLE)

..................................***'Engage in business*** *until I come.'*
(English Standard Version)

.....***Use this to earn more money*** *until I get back."*
(Contemporary English Vers)

....***Trade*** *with this till I come*
(New Jerusalem Bible)

Jesus is coming back...., but He has not yet returned. So
we are to do business with our giftings until He comes.
Locate your talent from the above groups and use it to
trade until He comes. *He is the head of the body and he has
given you a talent as a part of His body.* These are the practical
realities of increase. Once you have discovered your
purpose; it is easier to command value because you will be
in your element. After all fishes don't go to swimming
school.

Your purpose is directly related to what you love. *The most
purposeful people in the world spend their time doing what they*

love. Bill Gates loves computers, Oprah loves helping, and Edison loved to invent. What do you love? Is it reading, writing, playing sports, singing, painting, business, selling, talking, listening, cooking, fixing broken things. Whatever you love, it's directly related to your purpose.

> *"Your purpose is directly related to what you love. The most purposeful people in the world spend their time doing what they love"*

What you love reflects in what you do with your free time. Whatever you do in your free time is a sign of your purpose. If you like to paint in your free time, then that's a "sign." If you like to cook, then that's a sign, if you like to talk, then that's a sign. Follow the signs. I love to learn & solve problems in my free time, I have an obsession with learning. Of course, this is a sign of my purpose…which is to teach. What do you do in your free time? What would you like to do if you had more free time? Finally; what you spend your free time doing begin to determine what you notice easily. A salesman notices an uninspiring sales pitch, a hairdresser notices someone's hair is out of place, a designer notices a awkward outfit, a mechanic hears something wrong with your car, a singer notices when someone's voice is out of pitch, a speaker notices an uninspiring speech. What do you notice?

"What you love reflects in what you do with your free time. Whatever you do in your free time is a sign of your purpose"

To unlock divine provisions that eliminate financial hardship, you need to discover your talents (Purpose) and do business with it until He comes. Then you can command value as you do so. God bless you.

CHAPTER 6

What Determines
Value Perception

I want to quickly explain the five components of value perception. Value is not what something is really worth. But what people believe it is worth. The key element there is belief. Let us look at the kinds of value perception that exist.

1. HISTORICAL OR KNOWN VALUE: If I say I own a Ferrari at home for example, many of you will know what that means. I don't have to tell you, before you know that a Ferrari is an expensive car. How do you know that? It is because; it has always been an expensive car. It has a historical value that you know about. Such values are commonly known to people.

2. DECLARED OR SOLD VALUE: In other words, the value is what people are prepared to pay for it. Many times they would want to sell a painting; they will say maybe it would fetch a million. And by the time the sell it, somebody has paid twenty million for it. It means that the people selling the artwork themselves don't know the value. They only put an idea. And then the value becomes what it is actually sold for.

3.   IMPLIED VALUE: If as you open the door to go out of your house, you see a man in a Rolls Royce. And he came out wearing Rolex watch, top Italian shoes. What would be your immediate assumption when you see him? What will you imply from seeing him? That he is rich and wealthy of course. Whether he is truly rich or not is not the issue; but you implied that he is rich because of the way he has presented himself. It is important that sometimes there is a value perception that is due to the way you present

Yourself. And it is vital that you understand and appreciate this. Someone once said that if you want to be a millionaire, you must think like a millionaire. It sounds simple, but it is true. There are certain mentalities that you can never have and be a millionaire. It is not possible. For example, you need to accept that value is simply about price. The value of something to a person has all manner of dynamics and considerations involved.

"If you want to be a millionaire, you must think like a millionaire"

There is a story I read some months ago about an unemployed guy in the State of Atlanta in the US. He has been unemployed for about nine months and he was depleting his savings and could not get a job. So he thought; what was he going to do? He concluded that he was so desperate and needed to make it big. He did not want to do anything illegal of course. So with the last chunk of his savings, he went to register in the local golf course. His wife complained about his "irrational decision". But he persisted, knowing that majority of the club members were millionaires. So he thought if he was around them, something will rub off. Since he had no job; he was playing golf every day.

They had a schedule of who is coming to play each day. He looks for the names of all the big guys and when they are listed to play; he comes too to be on the course at the same time with them. And you know people talk business when they are playing golf. He was not playing with them; he was just in the vicinity hearing what they discussed. After three months, he maintained his routine of hanging around the big guys and as they were playing somebody mentioned an investment opportunity. One of the guys said to the others; *'why don't you buy XYZ stock, they are enlisting in a couple of weeks' time'*.

One of the guys answered and said since he was only going to make two million dollar from such deal, he was not interested in such a small opportunity. They were discussing but this man listened to them. He got back home; quickly went to borrow money and bought that stock and a month later he sold it. He made $3.2 million dollars on the stocks and options. Now what did he do to make that? He changed his mentality. He understood that to get something he has never got; he has to do something he has never done. He understood therefore that he needed to be in a particular kind of environment.

Similarly, if you go to a top restaurant, you could see that a bottle of coke cost £20. You are not paying for the coke in the restaurant because you can buy a coke in the supermarket for £1. But in this case; What you are paying for is the ambience, the environment, the company you will come in contact with, the prestige and so on. So what represents value to you should not just be about price; there are lots more to consider.

> *"To get something he has never got; he has to do something he has never done"*

But this is a problem for many folks I have encountered in the Church of God. To many of them; everything is about; how much is it? Do you know there are a few shops in Hollywood that their products don't have price tags. You go into the shop; pick what you want; it is when you get to the pay-point that they tell you the price. How many of you can shop there? There are some things money cannot buy. It is very important that you understand that there is what I call implied value.

4.   INFLUENCED VALUE: Influenced value is about impressions we have about people that is as a result of third party influence. If you have never heard or met a guest speaker before. And your pastor says XYZ person is coming as a guest minister; what your pastor says about that guy will influence your esteem and value of the guest before he arrives. Your value perceptions can be influenced. For example, if Oprah feature your book in her book show the sales of that book will skyrocket. Every time it has happened. So she has a kind of influence on the kind of book people read. This is influenced value.

5.   CULTURAL OR EXOTERIC VALUE: There are always cultural elements to value perceptions. What a culture consider as valuable could be seen as rubbish in another culture. It is very important to understand that people have cultural values. And within these cultural values, are social norms and believe systems. In an hierarchical society like Nigeria for instance; If certain famous religious leaders come into a place, instantly many ascribe high value to them. Even if you don't know them personally, but the fact that they occupy certain position, instantly, gives them certain level of instant value. Therefore there are values that are attached to positions and titles.

WHAT DETERMINES VALUE

What is it that determines the value people place on things or people? This is one of the areas I want us to explore. I call it the **12Ps of value.**

1.   PERSONAL CONFIDENCE

The first P is the value determined by personal confidence and belief. In other words, people will not give you value if you don't have confidence in your own value. Confidence is a major issue, the Bible says; *"do not cast away your confidence for it will be of great recompense of reward".* You project greater value the more confident you are about what you have. A good salesman is a confident salesman. He can sell anything to anybody. It is important for you to understand that you need confidence to project your value. And you as a child of God, need to begin to show absolute confidence. You might not have noticed this; but rich people walk in a particular way; confidence is written all over the way they walk.

"You project greater value the more confident you are about what you have"

Personal confidence is essential in an uncertain world where everybody is threatened; having personal confidence is a magnet. People are attracted to that kind of persons. Because you are have a calming effect on everybody. Personal confidence is one of the key determinants of value. Confidence can convince you, and as such, you can convince other people. It is therefore very important that personal confidence is seen as a determinant of value. Therefore, Personal confidence has the capability to project value on an individual than timidity.

2.   PRESENTATION

Second P of value is presentation. Value of something can be determined by its presentation. And that is why (except you are a manufacturer); items like gold and diamond are never sold to the general public in raw/dirty format; as it looks when it is first extracted. Because being rough and dirty, most people will not place the right value on the black dirty looking stones or buy it at its right value. It takes experts who know what it is to buy it in that state. Ordinary consumers then get the opportunity to buy after they have been cleaned and processed into shinning metals that now attract great value. This shows that presentation is key.

> *"Personal confidence has the capability to project value on an individual than timidity"*

How you present something can give it value or no value. You want to write a book and you went to print it in the backyard of your father's house. The texts can hardly be seen. You have diminished the value of that book regardless of its brilliant content. For example if any of you has ever bought any Apple product; one of the key thing Apple specializes in (as part of its value proposition) is packaging. The money Apple spends in their packaging is more than some other companies spend on their actual products. That is why you see many owners of Apple products keep the packaging for months and even years; while the same people when they buy other PCs, throwing away the bog standard packaging within days.

> *"How you present something can give it value or no value"*

3.   PRICE

The third determinant of value is price. The price of something can affect the value that you give it; although there are exceptions. Generally speaking; Price for some items is a determinant of value. So as a general rule; a car costing $50,000 is expected to be more valuable than a car costing $5,000. A suit that cost £1000 is expected to be more valuable than one that cost $70. Price however tends to be a revealer of other value composition. For example, Price can reveal a product has better longevity or better quality; so the price is not really the reason people buy such products; but price can help to reveal these other more important value containers.

"The price of something can affect the value that you give it; although there are exceptions"

4.   PURPOSE

The value of something also can be determined by its purpose or function. In other words, the more functional your gifting is, the better its value. Sometimes something that can provide one solution is cheaper that what can provide ten solutions. That is why multifunctional devises are better value to many people. Any product that solve multiple problems will as a general rule be more valuable than products that solve only one problem. Similarly, a medicine that cures cancer will be expected to be more valuable than one that cures headache. Why? Because a bigger functional benefit translates into bigger value proposition. So the purpose therefore matters.

> *"Any product that solve multiple problems will as a general rule be more valuable than products that solve only one problem"*

5.   PERCEPTION

Value is also determined by perception. In other words how people perceive you or perceive your services or products can determine the value people are prepared to place on it. If people associate your brand with quality, and they perceive that you always sell quality products, they are happy to pay the extra.

I was listening to the son of the man who owns the largest Toyota dealership in Nigeria – Elizade; at a meeting in early 2012. He was telling the seminar how they as committed Christians; decided that they will not cut corners in their business. So they pay ALL the duties due on the Toyota cars they sell; while they observe others bring in Toyota and cut corners with duty payments and do all manner of questionable stuff. As a result, their Toyota cars are about twenty five per cent more expensive than other dealers that sell Toyota. Yet their company is still the number one Toyota car seller in Nigeria. Why? Quality service perception and delivery. Because people understand that if you buy car from them, you will get top rate service and 100% original Toyota. So the extra people pay seem worth it to the customer.

> *" If people associate your brand with quality, and they perceive that you always sell quality products, they are happy to pay the extra"*

Perception can however be falsely created. This will work until the truth is found out. Every falsely created perception will eventually lead to collapse as it will not be sustainable in the long term. It is important therefore for you to understand that perception can affect value. So create the right perception for your product or service and you will see higher value placed on it by the customers.

> *"Every falsely created perception will eventually lead to collapse as it will not be sustainable in the long term"*

6.   PUBLICITY
Value is also determined by Publicity. Being gifted does

not automatically mean that you will be known for it. Those who better publicize their talent can secure better value for it. If Joseph did not speak to the butler, Pharaoh may not have known he was able to interpret dreams. It is important to understand that sometimes you need to publicize what you have got. You have to make known to the public what you have got otherwise; you may not secure correct value for it.

> *"Those who better publicize their talent can secure better value for it. If Joseph did not speak to the butler, Pharaoh may not have known he was able to interpret dreams"*

7.   PROMOTION

Value is also determined by promotion. In other words, you need to promote what you have. Promotion is about the message; publicity is about the medium. Publicity is about whether you are doing it through word of mouth, radio, newspaper or TV. But the actual message you are sending out is promotion. You need to learn to promote yourself. Nobody was there when you were called. So your value has to be promoted and publicized. You were alone with God when you received your vision; so how do you expect others (who were not there) to celebrate that vision if you don't make it known to them.

*"Promotion is about the message;
publicity is about the medium"*

*And I Daniel **alone** saw the vision: for the men
that were with me saw not the vision;...*

Daniel 10:7

It became the responsibility of Daniel to then publish the vision. The Lord gave the word; and great was the company of them that publish it. You have a responsibility to make known to the world what you received in private from God. Your gift, your purpose; your passion need to be made known to others to enjoy value for it.

*"Nobody was there when you were called.
So your value has to be promoted and
publicized"*

8.   PERSONALITY

Personality can drive or destroy value. Many people have the same gifts, but the personality of individuals can drive or destroy it's value. For example; If you think about what makes people beautiful to you, you will discover that it is more than their personality and not so much their look.

Looks can change. It is the personality that is actually key.

I remember in my secondary school (A Level) days, I would go to parties with my mates and when we met new girls; we debated which of us will chat her up. But on this particular occasion we agreed I should do it; but as I moved closer, the girl turned around and spoke to me. Instantly I lost interest. Why you may ask? She had the most horrible accent and terrible command of English language. The beauty was wonderful, but the moment she opened her mouth, the beauty disappeared. Physically she was still looking the same. But for me the attraction was instantly lost because she didn't have the personality that commanded or communicated value to me.

> *"Looks can change. It is the personality that is actually key".*

You need to understand that there is something called body language. When somebody speaks to you, research has shown that 88 to 90 per cent of what you understand about what they have said is not via the words they have spoken. Ninety per cent is about what I call **non-verbal communication**. Their tone of voice, my gesticulations, my body language, my facial expression; all those things are ways of communicating. It is therefore important that you have a personality to convey certain value. That is why if some people come into millions tomorrow, they will never look wealthy and will find it hard to command the value they deserve, despite their riches. But there are also people out there that are not wealthy; but have charming and charismatic personalities that command value way above their actual financial status.

> *"When somebody speaks to you, research has shown that 88 to 90 per cent of what you understand about what they have said is not via the words they have spoken"*

Personality matters a lot. You need to have the personality to carry the value that people project on you. That is why if you marry into the royal *family,* one of the first things you are taught is how to conduct yourself as a royal. So you need to learn to develop a personality that will command value.

9.   PROVISIONING

Value is also determined by provisioning. In other words the more investment you put into developing a talent, the more value that talent will be seen to have; all things being equal. If both of us have talent in music and I have never gone to music school, I have never made any investment in music. And here you are, you have gone to all the best schools, you have invested into music. Even though originally both of us have the talent, you will have more value than I, because you have invested more in it. You need to provide and invest in developing you talent.

10.   PARTNERSHIP

Values can also be determined by partnership. The Bible says *walk with the wise and you will be wise but the companion of fools shall be destroyed.* So sometimes forming the right alliances can determine whether your value is carrying through or not. That is why the bible says that iron sharpens iron. (Proverbs 27:17) You need to have the right partnership to make things work; since nobody succeed alone. The right relationships can propel your value to the next level.

> *"You need to have the right partnership to make things work; since nobody succeed alone"*

11.   PROLONGATION

Value is determined by prolongation and longevity or durability. In other words, the more durable an item or a product is, the more valuable it is. Don't be penny wise; pound foolish by buying products that are not durable. You need to bear in mind total cost of ownership; nut just the buying cost if you are to assess product value. How much will this cost me to maintain? What additional cost would I have spent in five years time? A shirt costing you $80 and lasting five years *is* a lot cheaper than a shirt costing you $10 that spoils after three months. So value given to a product or service can be determined by it durability. The longer a product lasts, the higher value it attracts.

> *"You need to bear in mind total cost of ownership; nut just the buying cost if you are to assess product value"*

12.   PHILANTHROPY.

Value can also be determined by philanthropy. Sometimes if a business idea or proposal is couched in philanthropic ways, or housed in philanthropic attire, it attracts more value. For example, people will give more if something is for charity. If there is an auction for charity, people will pay more. Also if you go to all the shops in US and Europe; you will find a range of products called Fair Trade products. It is more expensive because of the philanthropic element. Higher value can therefore be determined by philanthropy.

CHAPTER 7

Strategies To Commanding Value

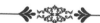

Now you know what determines value; but how do you command value. What are the prerequisites? I have come to understand that as believers; our lives have to conform to Godly principles and we have to go through defined paths to succeed in ways that bring glory to God.

STRATEGIES TO COMMANDING VALUE

1.   To command value, **you will need to have a dream or a vision**. Because the value of zero is zero. We cannot begin to talk of you commanding value, if you don't have a vision driven by Purpose. Because you have nothing to wrap your value around. Value is wrapped round purpose, as we have examined in a previous chapter.

2.   To command value, **you have to go through Process that will test and get rid of value killers in your life.** God will take you through the threshing floor. You are going to go through 'process' that will test you to the limits. Process or brokenness teaches us to trust God. We are taught submission and obedience to God. And when you are going through process, nothing works. You pray, you tithe; the mountain is still not moving. That is why the bible says *"having done all to stand, stand therefore."* Sometimes that is all you have to do. Just keep standing having done all you have to do; that mountain will eventually shift. God is taking you through a process. He has to prepare you for what he has prepared for you. And therefore need to understand that he will take you through process to command value.

God will take you through PROCESS. It is during process that God empties you of anything that mammon can use to gain a foothold in your life. Concerning Jesus, the bible reveals that He went through the same purging.

> *I will not talk with you much more, for the prince (evil genius, ruler) of the world is coming. And he has no claim on Me. [He has nothing in common with Me; **there is nothing in Me that belongs to him,** and he has no power over Me.]*
>
> John 14:30 (AMP)

Jesus said, there is nothing in me that belong to the devil. Can you say the same thing? This is why God will take you through Process and brokenness; to empty you of everything the enemy can use to destroy you. During Process, you will learn to imbibe Godly values and develop trust in God at all times. You will also learn not to trust in uncertain riches; but in God the great provider.

> *"It is during process that God empties you of anything that mammon can use to gain a foothold in your life"*

3.   To command value, **you have to learn to say no to temporal success as the price to obtain ultimate value.** Joseph could have become a top gun in Potiphar's house. But he rejected temporary elevation for ultimate value. So sometime you have to turn your back to what looks good in other to get the best. In Hebrew 11, the Bible talks about the hall of faith; By faith Abraham obtained this; by faith Moses obtained this; by faith Isaac obtained this, towards the end it now says, by faith *Moses refused to be called the son of Pharaoh's daughter.*

Then it hit me that we need faith to refuse. Not just faith to receive. If you don't have the faith to refuse, then your faith to receive will go nowhere. Why, because the devil knows how to open doors too. You will not need faith to refuse if what you are refusing is a bad thing. Being called the son of Pharaoh's daughter was one of the best things you could be called. It is like every single door has opened to you. And on the other hand, being a slave has no attraction whatsoever. So it took faith for him to turn his back on what looked good because he had to fulfil destiny. We need faith to refuse before our faith to receive can fully work. That is what I mean when I say you need to learn to say no to temporal success as a price to obtain ultimate value. If you have never had to say no to what looks good, you have not yet started your walk to kingdom abundance. Because the enemy will open doors very fast when he sees that you are on your way to destiny. And you have to learn not to enter those doors. The Bible says if possible, the very elect will be deceived. The very elect will not be deceived if the difference is obvious. You have to know how to sense counterfeit. So to command value; you have to pass through process; after which you are now ready to command value as God leads you.

> *"If you don't have faith to refuse, then your faith to receive will go nowhere"*

4.   To command value, **you must have Integrity to develop lasting value**. You cannot command what you don't have. You have to learn how to develop value through integrity. You know integrity is a big word and

there are different dimensions to it. But the important thing you need to understand is that a man of integrity sticks to his own words even to his ruin. The cunning, crafty, crooked business deals that promise much (but bring in little) do not belong to the man of integrity. The man of integrity gives his word and, by gum, come hell or high water, he will stick to it. Integrity and faithfulness go hand in hand. Integrity is heart honesty. Faithfulness is sticking to your word, no matter what may come your way.

The King of kings and Lord of lords is worthy to reign, and will reign. He is called, *"Faithful and True."* And the army that follows him on white horses are clothed in white, clean, fine linen (Revelation 19:11-14). Again, Revelation 17:14 describes those who follow the Lamb, *"These will make war with the Lamb and the Lamb will overcome them, for he is Lord of lords and King of kings; and those who are with him are called, chosen, and faithful."* Integrity will win in the end. All who despise it will lose. It is not enough to only admire the virtues of integrity. We must personally embrace it and possess it. Integrity is one of the great preservatives for the peril of our times.

- Psalm 25:21, *"Let integrity and uprightness preserve me."*
- Psalm 26:11, *"But as for me, I will walk in my integrity."*

- Psalm 41:12, *"As for me, you uphold me in my integrity."*

Integrity is a very precious jewel to those who realise its worth. For your Value Proposition to endure and become a legacy; it must be built on integrity.

> *"Integrity is heart honesty. Faithfulness is sticking to your word, no matter what may come your way"*

Job confesses, *"Till I die I will not put away my integrity from me"* (Job 27:5). What a powerful declaration to come from a man who was suffering such a vicious attack from Satan. God himself testifies about Job to Satan, *"Have you considered my servant Job, that there is none like him on the earth, a blameless and upright man, one who fears God and shuns evil" And still he holds fast to his integrity, although you incited me against him to destroy him without cause?"*

> *"For your Value Proposition to endure and become a legacy; it must be built on integrity"*

Oh how tempting it is to compromise integrity, even just a little, to get a good business deal, to get off a speeding ticket, or to squirm out of a criticism you may have spoken about someone. You desperately want to save your own face. Multitudes compromise integrity every day to get their way in lawsuits. Politics has now become a dirty word for lack of integrity. We are living in a world where compromise is considered a normal way of living. All I can say is this: if you have to compromise, even a little, make sure it is not your integrity. Do not throw integrity to the wind, no matter what you may have to lose to maintain it. To throw away your integrity is almost the same as throwing away your soul. Any value you build outside of integrity will fade and collapse sooner or later. Most of us have allowed our integrity to slide in one way or another at some time in our lives. It's not too late to repent. Ask for forgiveness, and pick it up again. Commit to integrity as a foundation to command trans-generational value.

> *"Do not throw integrity to the wind, no matter what you may have to lose to maintain it"*

Somebody once said that integrity is sticking to what you promise to do; long after the mood you were in when you said it has left you. It is therefore very important and absolutely crucial that we understand that we have to develop value through integrity. In other words, you must pass Mrs Portifer's test.

"Integrity is sticking to what you promise to do; long after the mood you were in when you said it has left you"

5.   To command value, you have to **invest in others and give value to others**. How do you procure value out of other people by investing in them? Here are a few ways to do so:

25 WAYS TO ADD VALUE TO PEOPLE

One of the key requirements to Command Value is that you add Value to others. The rules of life are such that you become what you give away. Below are just some of the many ways you can add Value to those you interact with and thus increase your ability to Command Value in life.

1.   Complement people in some way within the first 30 seconds of your conversation.

When you are meeting someone for the first time, or for the 100th time, it is always nice to speak kind and complimentary words! Notice that the person looks happy or acknowledge a recent accomplishment of theirs; people are always looking for acceptance, make someone feel valued by noting their specialness in the form of a sincere compliment!

_____

_____

_____

_____

"The rules of life are such that you become what you give away"

2. Ask people questions about three key areas: their passions, their projects, and their principles.

Begin a conversation with, "I value your opinion about _____(subject ideas: class, school, church) that I am thinking of joining, could you share your thoughts on it with me?" It is a positive way to make someone feel as though you hold their opinions in high regard. It is an intimate look into the person to whom you are speaking. Because the question is open ended you may learn a lot about a topic of interest to you both, as well as a lot about the person!

_____

_____

_____

_____

3. Complement a person about something specific *in front of* another person.

This one is tricky, be careful not to say, "Wow I haven't seen you in a while, you have lost a lot of weight!" This has happened in my presence before! I was with a new friend who ran into an old friend while we were all at a game. My poor friend was very embarrassed! Clearly, you can find a nice complement to say to someone that will not mortify them!

_____

_____

_____

_____

4.   Remember people's names.

This is a big tip when dealing with people in business. People are very attached to their name! Nothing makes a person feel valued more than knowing they made enough of an impression on you for you to remember their name! It helps in the dating world, too!

_____

_____

_____

_____

5.   Remember people's birthdays, anniversaries, and special occasions. Send them a note on those dates to let them know you are sharing in their celebration.
It doesn't matter if a person is 4 or 40, everyone likes to be acknowledged for being born! If you can make a note in your records of someone's birthday and remember to send a card or make a surprise phone call on their special day you will surely make them feel valued! Same goes for life events such as anniversaries!

_____

_____

_____

_____

6.   Strive to be the first to help a person whom you know in need Sometimes we can be at the right place, at the right time, for someone who needs our assistance! You know when those moments happen and you act on them, most of the time! Have you ever reached to the top shelf for an elderly lady at the grocery store and graciously smiled when she thanked you? If yes, you most certainly made her feel valued! Keep your eyes and heart open for ways to be helpful in your family and your community. Making another person feel valued will make you feel valued as well!

_____

_____

_____

_____

7.   Help people focus on their strengths and assist them in delegating their weaknesses

Most people buy into the notion that they need to work on their weaknesses. But they will be most valuable in the area of their strengths. If a person is good at organizing, give them responsibilities in that area. Let them use their unique giftedness to accomplish a task in their way. If a person struggles in the area of public speaking, putting them up in front of people may only frustrate them.

People will feel more valuable to an organization or team when they are able to do things that they're good at. In school, when a parent looks at their student's report card, their attention seems to be focused on the lower grades. "You have to get those up," they might say.

Unfortunately, many people live with this sense of always having to focus on our weaknesses instead of being recognized for and honouring our strengths. While it's important to get good grades and do your best, no one gets straight A's in life. There will always be things that we're better at than other things.

8. Smile at people. Smile when you talk to them. Smile when you walk by them

Smiles are contagious and free! Some people will wonder what is so funny, or what you are up to! Isn't that worth it? You can give a stranger a smile and possibly make their whole day brighter! What have you got to lose? Remember: a smile is free; and your day goes the way of the corners of your mouth!

_____

_____

_____

_____

9. When someone asks for your help or assistance with something, always do a little bit extra. It is the extra that turns ordinary into extraordinary

This is called "going the extra or second mile." It means we have the opportunity to do more than is expected of us. It is the "and then some" mindset. Someone asks you to help them clean their backyard, so you help them clean their backyard and then some other parts of their house. Zig Ziglar notes that there "isn't much traffic on the second mile" – not very many travel there. This is why it shows people how much you value them when you make the extra effort for them.

_____

_____

_____

_____

10.   Spend time with people. Often we communicate a person's value to them simply because we like hanging out with them, even if there's no agenda

Time is a precious commodity and a valuable resource. How can you spend this resource effectively on others? I remember being at a wedding where the best man gave a speech that told how he knew the moment that his best friend had met his future wife. He said that he and his best friend had been inseparable from Kindergarten through college, and then along came Kate! He said that his friend told him one day, "She is my favourite person in the world to just hang out with. No offense, buddy!" The reception hall filled with laughter as we knew the groom was expressing love for Kate to his best friend without trying to insult him. Being the person that someone just wants to hang out with is an amazing feeling...our free time is truly the only thing that most of us have to give to another person, and it is the most precious gift of all. Who do you show their value to by "just hanging out" with them?

_____

_____

---

11.   Add value to your own life. By doing this, you'll always have something to add to the lives of others

My favourite illustration in this area is found in the standard airline safety talk. When flight attendants stand in front of the semi-coherent, yet captive audience, they will often say, "In case of a loss of cabin pressure, oxygen masks will fall from the ceiling. Place the mask over your nose and mouth...if you are travelling with a child (or someone who is acting like a child) be sure to put your mask on FIRST before assisting your child." This is an important point. If you're not breathing, you can't assist anyone else. The same is true in our own growth – if you're not growing, you don't really have anything to add to someone else's growth. Focus on your own growth.

"If you're not breathing, you can't assist anyone else. The same is true in our own growth – if you're not growing, you don't really have anything to add to someone else's growth. Focus on your own growth".

12. Many people are well-equipped to point out problems. Help identify solutions for others who can't seem to work through their difficulties

Don't put up with complainers by joining in. Whenever someone comes to me with a problem, I ask them what solutions they have considered. By doing this, I force them to think strategically about the problem. Sometimes another person already knows what should be done, they just need confirmation. But if a person hasn't considered any solutions, I don't want to do all the thinking for them. When another person approaches you with a problem, ask them what solutions they've thought of. If they haven't thought of any, you might want to guide them through a problem-solving exercise on this occasion. Then encourage them to do it on their own before they approach you with a problem the next time.

13.   Delegate tasks to other people in the area of your strengths; not just area of weakness. Follow-up on their progress and praise them for a job well done

People like to do things they are good at. As a leader, some people are sometimes timid to delegate tasks in areas where they are weak and didn't necessarily enjoy the work. They may wonder to themselves, "There's no way someone else will want to do this." But how wrong they are. Someone else may enjoy and actually like doing this kind of thing and is good at it and...even have fun with it.

_____

_____

_____

_____

14.   Always bring something to the table - whether it's resources, ideas, or opportunities

Bring a book, an article, even a good quote. Sometimes it is extra special when you combine your presence with some presents. When you give someone something that will help them grow personally, it tangibly communicates your desire to invest in that person.

_____

_____

_____

_____

15. Share your knowledge with others. Don't keep your best ideas and strategies all to yourself

People used to assume that knowledge was power. If I knew more than you, then I had some type of power over you. But I don't want to have power over you, I want to add value to you. So I share my best stuff. I give it away. When I discover something (a new tool, a new strategy, a new idea), I pass it on. This is the whole premise of Web 2.0. Make it free. If you pass it on to others and it's good stuff you'll discover a whole new kind of power - the power of appreciation.

_____

_____

_____

_____

"If you pass it on to others and it's good stuff you'll discover a whole new kind of power - the power of appreciation"

16. Don't view people as they are but as who they have the potential to become. Do your best to draw the very best out of people

Teachers and Business Managers have to do this everyday, don't they? That is why good teachers call themselves, "facilitators of learning". If you look at yourself as a facilitator of valuing others, you cannot help but to draw the best out of people. Toss the proverbial softball to someone who you know needs to hit one out of the park! Help someone get back into the game by stoking their flame, not by intimidating them! It is great to be on a team with people who recognize the need to be respected for the person they are striving to become! I had a boss/trainer once that never beat us up about mistakes that we made at work; he would just outline the issue, suggest the solution for the future action and end the brief meeting with, "Now get back to work, My Champions! (Because of his understanding approach he is my favourite boss to this day!)

_____

_____

_____

_____

17. Catch somebody doing something right and praise them for it in front of others whom you'd like to see exhibit similar behaviour

This is such a great piece of advice for all of us; whether we are teachers, managers, or moms and dads! How can you celebrate someone's value; by putting them on a pedestal for a job well done?

_____

_____

_____

_____

18.   Develop an energetic greeting when you see people

This is a great suggestion...you do not have to be the cheerleader-type to muster up a sincere smile and a twinkle in your eye when you greet someone! I don't think that most people realize how validating it is to get a warm greeting from someone! You do not have to go "French" with the kiss kiss ritual, but you really can and should show some jubilation when you are greeting people. Show some spunk and people will be happy to see you too!

_____

_____

_____

_____

19.   Create mementos of special occasions that you spend with people.

Hey guys...want to score some major points with the ladies? Of course you do! Try grabbing a matchbook on your way out of the door of a restaurant when you are on a date. If you are non-smoker (and I pray that you are!) your date may ask, "Why are you taking matches, you don't smoke, do you?" and then you get to be smooth-guy and respond with the value-packed: "Ahhh, you caught me! I just wanted to remember tonight's date with YOU!" Girls admire a guy who think that they are worth remembering! Now be sure to call her the next day and to call her by the correct name! If you can hang onto that matchbook until your honeymoon; well, then you are gold!

20. Keep people accountable to their promises, goals, and commitments

When you care about someone enough to point out to them that a commitment that they have made is not being met, you are a friend that is trying to show the other person how valuable you think they are to that commitment **and to you**.

21. Be sincere in your sincerity. Sincerity is something that you cannot fake

This is the true difference between adding value to someone else and trying to sell them something! We all have a sincerity meter inside of us and we can detect a salesman three blocks away, can't we? Adding value to someone else is a pure and sincere gesture. If you are not "feeling it", neither will the other person! Try your best to do the selfless favour without any other motivation…your sincerity will shine through!

_____

_____

_____

_____

"We all have a sincerity meter inside of us and we can detect a salesman three blocks away, can't we? Adding value to someone else is a pure and sincere gesture"

22. Make eye contact. Look them square in the eye. Make a note of their eye colour

I have a hard time believing someone who is talking to me and not LOOKING at me ! Don't you? I can always tell when one of my children is "fibbing" because their eyes look away from mine while they are talking. The eyes are the window to the soul, someone once said, and I believe this to be true. When you are talking to someone, let your soul shine through those windows of yours! Eye contact will let the person that you are talking to know that: a) you value their opinion of you, and b) you stand behind what you are saying!

_____

_____

_____

_____

> *"Eye contact will let the person that you are talking to know that: a) you value their opinion of you, and b) you stand behind what you are saying"*

23.   Have a positive attitude in all situations.

An attitude is contagious. If you have a positive attitude you will influence those around you who may be tempted to be negative. Decide to be a thermostat rather than a thermometer. A thermometer measures and reflects the current temperature. A thermostat is used to set the temperature you want.

_____

_____

"Decide to be a thermostat rather than a thermometer. A thermometer measures and reflects the current temperature. A thermostat is used to set the temperature you want"

24. Pray for someone.

No matter what your spiritual level is, there is a deep, spiritual value in praying for other people. Pray specifically for them and for their needs. You know that there is serious power in prayer for both the prayer and the prayee! Try it right now...think of someone that needs a prayer, close your eyes, recite your heartfelt sentiment and experience the feeling of compassion that comes over you. It is a sensation like none other. You may want to tell the person for whom you are praying that they are in your prayers; but it is amazing.

"No matter what your spiritual level is, there is a deep, spiritual value in praying for other people"

25.   Adding value to people is a daily decision, not something that you do in a day.
It takes time, effort, and sacrifice. Sometimes a person may resist your efforts for any number of reasons. Don't give up. Your decision to add value to people is not dependent upon someone's willingness to accept it. If they refuse, smile and invest in someone else.

_____

_____

_____

_____

"Your decision to add value to people is not dependent upon someone's willingness to accept it. If they refuse, smile and invest in someone else"

The list is there for you to practice with. Joseph helped others to interpret their own dreams before his own came to fruition.

6.   To command value, you have to **dress for where**

you are going, not where you are coming from. If I am in a first class cabin of an airplane, and the richest man in the world is next to me on that flight, I could have borrowed the money to pay for that flight, but as far as he is concerned, we are on the same class. That is the default assumption. That is why; he will give me access to him on that flight more readily than if I go to meet him in the office. You understand that we are on the same cabin, and if he paid what I paid, then we can talk. Automatically, he is projecting certain values on you, which may even be far from where you are in reality. That is why you are able to have access where ordinarily you won't. I remember some of the times I flew with many of the Nigerian Governors, the moment we enter Lagos, while the rest of us join the queue, from the plane, they whisk them to a car on the tarmac and they disappear.

> *"Joseph helped others to interpret their own dreams before his own came to fruition"*

But for the six hours on that plane there was no protocol and access to them was easy. It is vital to appreciate that to command value, you need to dress for where you are going not where you are coming from. People will always judge you by how you dress and present yourself. So it is important for you to allow your destination to inform your appearance if you are going to command value. If you are attending a meeting of company CEOs; you need to dress appropriately if you are not going to be seen as the driver or janitor when you enter. People will profile you on seeing you and immediately put you in a category in their mind. To command value you need to present yourself in a way that others will put you in the valuable box in their mind.

To command value and endure, **you have to give God the centre stage in everything.** Your obedience has to be total. 98% obedience is still disobedience. A little poison, poisons the whole fruit; so it is important to fully obey God's instructions. Obeying God in this respect may also mean, we might have to offload some unwise relationship. Until Abraham offloaded Lot, he did not hear God's voice afresh. Isaiah was a very good friend of King Uzziah, they were relations. But king Uzziah had such a stronghold on Isaiah that he could not hear God clearly in the first five chapters. But suddenly in chapter six of the book of Isaiah, the bible says: *In the year that King Uzziah died, I saw the Lord, high and exalted, seated on a throne; and the train of his robe filled the temple. (NIV)*

> *"To command value you need to present yourself in a way that others will put you in the valuable box in their mind"*

Now prior to Uzziah dying he couldn't see much. In some of our lives, Uzziah has to die. Everything that represents Uzziah in your life, I prophesy today they will die in Jesus Name. Amen! In that way you can be able to hear God and see God afresh. Isaiah said "I saw the Lord and His glory filled the temple". The Lord was there all along but he couldn't see God, perceive God because of the hold Uzziah had over him. We have to give God centre stage in our lives to be able to command real value.

> *"Your obedience has to be total. 98% obedience is still disobedience. A little poison, poisons the whole fruit; so it is important to fully obey God's instructions"*

7.   To command value, you need to have **a plan that will see you through the future.** Do you know that in the seven years of plenty, it was not only plentiful in Egypt, it was plentiful everywhere. The only reason why the whole world were coming to Egypt in the seven years of famine is that Egypt was the only nation that made provision during the seven years of plenty, when the rest did nothing. You need to understand therefore that to command value; you need to have a plan that will see you through the future. The very first war mentioned in the Bible was the battle of

the kings that Abraham fought to rescue Lot. And the Bible says; "when he heard that the kings have taken Lot", in the book of Genesis and the bible says; "and Abraham took his trained men of war". And I stopped there when I was reading the scripture because I now looked back, there was no war up until that time. Where did he get trained men of war from? He was training them for war in the time of peace. He was ever ready. He may never need them, but he had them trained. In other words, it is better to have what you don't need than to need what you don't have. So you need to have a plan that will see you through the future. You might not need every single element of the plan but without a plan, you are in trouble.

> *" It is better to have what you don't need than to need what you don't have"*

8.   To command value, you have to be able to **see value in people and respect the grace on their lives**. Joseph did not judge the baker and the butler, but he befriended them. You have to be able to see value in people, why; because the vehicle God will use to meet your needs is a human being. And you cannot attract into your life what you do not respect. You cannot expect God to use a vessel to meet your needs that you have desecrated. That is what God was telling Abraham when he said "they that bless you, I will bless and he that curse you I will curse". What this was

telling Abraham was that whoever sees my blessings on your life and bless you in return, I will assume they want the same blessings and I will give it to them. But whoever despises you because of my blessings on your life, I will assume they don't want the blessing, and I will deny them.

Truth: you cannot attract into your life who you don't respect. It is therefore important that you are careful how you see things. That brother came to church in a brand new car, rather than going round saying is he the first one to drive a brand new car; well he might not be the first one, but which one are you driving. If you begin to despise people because of the grace of God in their lives, you are more or less telling God; don't give me the same thing. It is important that you learn to see value in people.

> *"The vehicle God will use to meet your needs is a human being"*

9.   To command personal value, **you have to learn forgiveness and letting go of the past.** Joseph forgave his brothers, and he even named his first child Forget. Because he forgot, he was able to name the second one; for God has made me fruitful in the land of my affliction. You cannot be fruitful till you forget your past. To command value, you have to learn forgiveness and letting go of the past.

10. To command value, **you must possess some practical gifting.** Joseph did not administer Egypt by dreaming, the only way he was able to administer Egypt was that he was a very good manager of humans and resources. He wrote a manual on how to manage people. Even though the dream gave him assess, he was not dreaming every day for seven years. To administer Egypt, he needed to have some practical skills and gifting. It is important to note that there should be some element of practical skills not just all about spiritual. He dreamt, understood what he needed to do and then uses his practical skill to deliver.

11. To command value, **you need to think and act with posterity in mind.** In other words, Joseph worked on his legacy and secured a future for his generation. We live in a eat and die generation where many people don't care about what happens to the future generation. True value endures. Things and products that transcend generations are the true carriers of value. What are you going to leave behind once you are out of here? That is why the Bible says; "a good name is better than silver and gold". Because it gives you access to places money cannot buy. What are you going to leave for your children? Are your children going to suffer long after you or repeat all your mistakes? Or is it going to be a case of 'who is your father…really… we do not want to have anything to do with you; so now

your children are suffering for what their father did. Or is your name going to open doors for your children?

> *"True value endures. Things and products that transcend generations are the true carriers of value. What are you going to leave behind once you are out of here?"*

12.   To command value, **you must be prepared to be a loner for a season.** In other words you must develop a crowd resistance mentality. You must develop a crowd resistant mentality, and be prepared that a lot of lies will be written about you. Especially in the era of modern technology. The thing about Internet is that anyone could open a blog today and put on it that Pastor so so and so is a thief and a robber. The way Google (search engine) work is that it crawls all over the net collecting data and key words and names every day. Within three four days, if someone searches that Pastor's name, that blog will come up because Google has marched and achieved your name and thief together. Henceforth, when anybody searches your name, one of the results that will come up in Google is Pastor so so and so...is a thief. And people will click on the result and see it. The thing about the website is that anything can be said about anybody, with no regard for the truth.

That is why teachers will tell you in the university, don't use the Internet as an authority, don't even quote it, because half of the information there is untrue and some are outright rubbish. It is important for you to understand that anything can be said about you. And if you are constantly worrying about how people will see you, what they will write about you, you will not be able to be bold enough to create lasting value and succeed. The Bible says that *"if our hearts condemn us not we have confidence with God",* (1John 3:21). The issue here is about your relationship with God and as long as that is intact, it does not matter what people say, it does not matter what people write. We cannot be too conscious of what people write, they will write whatever they want.

I was with one of the Nigerian business gurus when he got a phone call that a prominent Nigerian newspaper that day wrote that he has been arrested by EFCC (Nigeria Anti-Corruption police unit) and that he is currently in custody. I was with the man sitting down and having breakfast. This is a man who has nothing to do with the EFCC. The newspaper carried it that currently, he is in custody. What do you say to a story like that? That will be on the newspaper's website. When you now search the guy's name you will see arrested, EFCC and his name linked in Google. It has to get to a point that you have to close your eyes and ears to all these things and understand that it is only one person that has sent you on an errand. And it is only Him that you are here to please. You have to develop a crowd resistant mentality. That is why we say that one with God is majority.

> *"If you are constantly worrying about how people will see you, what they will write about you, you will not be able to be bold enough to create lasting value and succeed"*

You cannot create true value if you are constantly trying to please people or be in everybody's good book. Value creation sometimes involves acting on your convictions rather than popular opinion. The main market research that was done for Apple before the release of the iPhone concluded that it will not sell as people don't want a phone without a keypad. Steve Jobs said he wanted to release iPhone for his own satisfaction even if nobody buys it. Now we see that his conviction paid off. People changed their views when they saw the actual item in the shops. The rest as they say is history. Same happened when Walt Disney was looking for backing for his cartoon characters. He was told it will not work. He wrote that he wanted to do the project more after he was told it would not work. He followed his conviction and not popular opinion. Therefore creating value will require you to be sometime unpopular or a loner. You must be confident in your God given conviction and trust Him for the outcome.

"Value creation sometimes involves acting on your convictions rather than popular opinion"

Child of God; you have all it takes to command value in your generation. So, what is God's final verdict concerning you? Here it is:

"They will build houses and inhabit them; they will also plant vineyards and eat their fruit. They will not build and another inhabit, they will not plant and another eat; for as the lifetime of a tree, so will be the days of My people, and My chosen ones will wear out the work of their hands. "They will not labour in vain, or bear children for calamity; for they are the offspring of those blessed by the LORD, and their descendants with them."

Isaiah 65:21-23

God does not begin what He has not already finished. So you need to be confident in God's Leadership of your life as you surrender to Him. God has already finished your journey and Isaiah 65 is His verdict from the beginning. So who can God use? ANYBODY.

Abraham Lincoln one of the most popular and most effective president in the United States failed in business at thirty-one years of age, was defeated for a legislative post at thirty-three. He failed again at business at thirty three, elected into legislature at thirty four, his wife died at thirty five, he had nervous breakdown at forty-three he was defeated for congress at forty six, he was defeated for congress again at forty eight. He was then elected as United States President at fifty one. What does that tell you; To never give up. It does not matter where you have been, how much defeat you have had, how big the wave is. No storm lasts forever, even tsunami will end. Stay where God has put you and allow God to bring you to his own wealthy place.

> *"It does not matter where you have been, how much defeat you have had, how big the wave is. No storm lasts forever, even tsunami will end"*

CHAPTER 8

The Spiritual Imperative
Of Commanding Value

There is a book I read few years ago titled: What they don't teach you at Harvard Business School; by Mark McCormack. It was a very interesting book, which more or less explained that sometimes if you dogmatically follow what you are thought in the academic concept, you find out that it is actually the major source of your problems. The thing with academics sometimes is that because you are taught to follow certain logic, you follow and the enemy is waiting for you at those gates. The Bible says that God will use the foolish things of this world to confound the wise. That means doing things that don't follow natural rules, sometimes. And that is where many of us run into challenges.

"And when the woman saw that the tree was good for food, and that it was pleasant to the eyes,

*and a tree to be desired to make one wise, she took of the fruit thereof, and did eat, and gave also unto her husband with her; and he did eat. [7] And the **eyes of them both were opened**, and they knew that they were naked; and they sewed fig leaves together, and made themselves aprons".*

- Genesis 3: 6-7

Now first question is; were they blind? Which eyes were opened? We need to begin to see things differently, if we are to succeed in strategically invading the marketplace and create value. I am going to be hammering on this issue of strategically invading the marketplace, because I believe that is the final frontier. That is the bit that the church has yet to understand how to conquer. And this is why it looks like the enemy has put all his resources in defending the marketplace. Because whoever control the marketplace will control the destiny of nations. So you cannot just stumble into commanding value in the marketplace purely with natural skill and knowledge alone. You cannot just stumble into it with MBA or PhD. There must be things that distinguish you in the marketplace that the enemy does not know how to comprehend. And that is the element that is missing in many of our lives which is why, on a day-to-day basis, I meet believers who stumble into business and stumble out very quickly.

Much research has shown repeatedly in the last ten years that the failure rate among Christians in business is the highest. And we need to understand why that is the case. We need to understand what is going on. Because it is not that they (Christians in business) are not qualified; in fact they are on paper at least most of the time. So why is it that if you go round you will find out that most of our people are the most qualified in their offices, yet they are the least paid. Their bosses don't have half their qualifications. If you don't look into the eyes of the spirit, and begin to see what is going on and how God has put systems in place to overcome it, you will just join a rat race and be struggling week on week.

> [12] *And one of his servants said, None, my lord, O king: but Elisha, the prophet that is in Israel, telleth the king of Israel the words that thou speakest in thy bedchamber.* [13] *And he said, Go and spy where he is, that I may send and fetch him. And it was told him, saying, Behold, he is in Dothan.* [14] *Therefore sent he thither horses, and chariots, and a great host: and they came by night, and compassed the city about.* [15] *And when the servant of the man of God was risen early, and gone forth, behold, an host compassed the city both with horses and chariots. And his servant said unto him, Alas, my master! how shall we do?*

[16] And he answered, Fear not: for they that be with us are more than they that be with them. [17] And Elisha prayed, and said, LORD, I pray thee, **open his eyes, that he may see.** *And* **the LORD opened the eyes of the young man;** *and he saw: and, behold, the mountain was full of horses and chariots of fire round about Elisha. [18] And when they came down to him, Elisha prayed unto the LORD, and said, Smite this people, I pray thee, with blindness. And he smote them with blindness according to the word of Elisha.*

- 2Kings 6:12-18

The background of the story here is that the Syrian army besieged the prophet and the servant was very afraid. Because all the servant could see was that they were surrounded by the army of Syria and he did not know what to do. He was afraid that they were going to be killed. The prophet prayed the prayer here that I want to link to Genesis Chapter three. He prayed a prayer in verse 17: *"And Elisha prayed and said Lord, open his eyes that he may see"*. Again I ask, was he blind? Can you see the connecting with Genesis 3 here yet? He said open his eyes that he could see. Then the Lord opened the eyes of the young man and he saw and behold the mountain was full of horses and chariots of fire all around Elisha's residence. The guy of course became bold from that moment onwards. What am

I saying here? We all have physical eyes as well as spiritual eyes. Your response in life will depend on which eyes you are using to look.

In Genesis 1: 26 the Bible says *"God created man in His image and His likeness"*. He pronounced to that man, be fruitful multiply and have dominion and replenish the earth and all that. That man in Genesis chapter one had no physical body. It was a spiritual man that God was speaking to. Because we see that it was not until Genesis chapter two, that God then formed a physical shape called man. He now put that man in Genesis chapter one; (the spiritual man he created), into that physical body and man became a living soul. The key point is this; the man that was created in Genesis chapter one was a spiritual man. He was the one that was supposed to have dominion. By the time the spiritual man was put into the physical clay, he retained his spiritual eyes, ears etc. That is why he was able to see God physically. When they fellowshipped, he was able to see God physically but because the spiritual controls the natural, he was also able to see into the natural as well. With the spiritual eyes he was able to see both into the spirit and into the physical.

Now the Bible says; "when they ate the fruit, their eyes became opened". What that simply meant was that their physical eyes became opened and their spiritual eyes became shut. So they could no longer see into the spirit realm. That was the beginning of limitation. From that moment onwards, man could no longer see into the spirit. All he could see was the physical thing and the very first thing he saw was that he was naked. Even though that he was naked all along.

> *"We all have physical eyes as well as spiritual eyes. Your response in life will depend on which eyes you are using to look"*

What does that mean? It means as you go about your activities in the marketplace and trying to command value; what do you see. Which eyes are you using to see things? Because if you keep using the physical eyes, all you are going to see is limitation, difficulty. What eyes are you using to see? Just like the servant of the prophet, the guy was so afraid he thought that they were about to die. But the moment his spiritual eyes were opened, he realized that between them and the enemy's army were chariots ready to deal with the enemy. So suddenly, he became bold. What was the difference? It was what he was able to see. A man believes what he is able to see more than what he hears. Any man believes what he sees than what he hears. What you see is what dictates what you believe. What you believe will dictate what you will become. We believe more what we see than what we hear.

> *"A man believes what he is able to see more than what he hears"*

The question then is what are you seeing? The prayer you need to pray for yourself is "Lord I want my eyes to be opened". Not that you are blind, but you want to begin to see what God sees. Because if we begin to see what God sees, many of the battles we have lost we will not loose. Many of the battles we run away from, we will not run away from it. So the spiritual imperative of commanding value is that we must be able to see from the eyes of the spirit to avoid the limitations and obstacles the enemy will bring our way. If you see only from the natural eyes; you will not be able to act on your convictions, as you should. You will also be limited to logic and common sense you are taught in college. Anyone who knows anything about God will know that He is not logical and many times He does not make sense. So to command value you need the capacity to see beyond the obvious.

> *"The spiritual imperative of commanding value is that we must be able to see from the eyes of the spirit to avoid the*

limitations and obstacles the enemy will bring our way"

CHAPTER 9

Economic
Signs of The End Times

The bible makes it clear that the rapture will take place before the tribulation. While we don't know yet the time for that, we know that there are signs that signposts the season. I want us to look at a few facts we need to be familiar with in the days we live in; this is what I call the economic signs of the end times.

> *"We have also a more sure word of prophecy; whereunto ye do well that ye take heed, as unto a light that shineth in a dark place, until the day dawn, and the day star arise in your hearts"*
> — 2 Peter 1: 19

It says we have the prophetic word confirmed. What are the things that confirm the prophetic word of what is going to happen in the last days. Let us look at some of them.

1.   **THERE WILL BE EXPLOSION OF THE USE OF MODERN TECHNOLOGY** as the end time approaches.

> *"He was granted power to give breath to the image of the beast, that the image of the beast should both speak and cause as many as would not worship the image of the beast to be killed.* [16] *He causes all, both small and great, rich and poor, free and slave, to receive a mark on their right hand or on their foreheads,* [17] *and that no one may buy or sell except one who has the mark or the name of the beast, or the number of his name".*
>
> Rev.13: 15 – 17

He causes all both small and great, rich and poor, free and slave, to receive a mark in their right hand or on their forehead. What is the scripture saying? It means that there will be a gradual emergence of the cashless society. This is one of the things that will happen as the last days draw near. I was reading an article recently by the CEO of visa Europe, and he said *"Retailers will soon begin to charge people for paying by cash".* It is true, that is the way things are going. The so called cashless thing is so predominant now that both countries that have the infrastructure to support it and those that don't have like Nigeria are all rushing their heads with compulsory cashless policies. For a long time before the Lord showed me some of these things I used to think and joke then, like a decade ago. I would say things like; *don't worry the end is near, I would just leave Europe and go back to Africa. I said because the anti-Christ will take some time to get there.* I joked that he will be functioning very well in the West first before he gets to Africa. I said this because our infrastructure is so bad that he won't want to stay there. But given what is happening in Africa now; it is almost as if there will be no difference.

Whether there is infrastructure or not, African governments all want cashless as well. You need to understand therefore that the explosion of modern technology is one of the signs of the last days. And what all this is needed for is to facilitate the centralised control needed during the tribulation period. That is the whole essence of these things. The central theme of what will happen during the tribulation is centralized control.

A very good example of the centralized control is already happening in the west already. If you wake up tomorrow, in the UK and you have a piece of land and wish to plant corn for instance. Do you know that you cannot just get the seed anywhere in the UK? You have to apply to ministry of agriculture to buy seed; so everything is centralized already in some respects. But thank God in Africa, we can still plant our corn easily and get our seed from anywhere.

The point I am making is that centralized control is the hallmark of the tribulation period. Therefore, society is gradually moving in that direction and people will support it not knowing what they are supporting as logical arguments are produced by the state to support the centralisation drive.

> *"You need to understand therefore that the explosion of modern technology is one of the signs of the last days. And what all this is needed for is to facilitate the centralised control needed during the tribulation period"*

2.   The second economic sign of the end times is that **THERE WILL BE POLARIZATION OF PROSPERITY AND POVERTY.** In other words the gap between the rich and the poor will increase. There will be complete decimation of the middle class. The rich will be richer and the poor will be very poor. Presently, the top two per cent of the world population owns about sixty per cent of the world's wealth. And that gap will increase over time.

> *And when he had opened the third seal, I heard the third beast say, Come and see. And I beheld,*

and lo a black horse; and he that sat on him had a pair of balances in his hand. ⁶ And I heard a voice in the midst of the four beasts say, A measure of wheat for a penny, and three measures of barley for a penny; and see thou hurt not the oil and the wine.

- Revelation 6: 5 – 6

3.   THERE WILL BE PRIORITY OF OIL IN THE MIDDLE EAST. The issue of oil in the Middle East will become very central. Seventy-five per cent of the world oil reserve is in either a country that is Islamic or hates Israel. It is important for you to understand that it will be a major issue in the days we are in and the one to come.

4.   PREOCCUPATION WITH MONEY AND MATERIAL THINGS. 2Timothy 3:1-2, the Bible says *"but know this that in the last days, perilous times will come for men will be lovers of themselves and lovers of money…."*. Then the list went on in terms of boastful, proud, disobedience to parents, unthankful and all that. There would be a major emphasis on material acquisition in the last day. And if care is not taken, that will affect the church as well. In fact it is already affecting the church some would say. And that is why you need to understand that the wealth of the wicked the bible says **"is stored up for the just"** not for **the church.** It is an individual thing. It is not the church that will come into divine wealth; it is individuals that will come into divine wealth but the Church will see its effect. And why is it so? Because you see clearly in Jeremiah 5:26 the bible says *"and among my people are found wicked men...."*.

So there are wicked people in church as well. That is why God will not take from the wealth of the wicked and give to the wicked. He takes from the wicked and gives to the just not the church. There are so many definitions of the wicked in scripture and naturally many of us think that the wicked is somebody who is not saved. While this is true, the biblical definition is much wider than that. For instance; what did the master call that servant that hid his one talent – wicked. So there are people in the church who are not utilizing the gift God has given them; they are equally wicked. The point is that there will be a preoccupation with money and material things in the last days.

5. THERE WILL BE PASSIVE INDIFFERENCE TO THE WARNING OF GOD. Just like in the days of Noah, many people will not take the warnings of God seriously. Some will even think you are stupid for trying to stick with what God is saying. It is important for us to see that many are already doing so.

"And as it was in the days of Noah, so it will be

also in the days of the Son of Man: [27] *They ate, they drank, they married wives, they were given in marriage, until the day that Noah entered the ark, and the flood came and destroyed them all.* [28] *Likewise as it was also in the days of Lot: They ate, they drank, they bought, they sold, they planted, they built;* [29] *but on the day that Lot went out of Sodom it rained fire and brimstone from heaven and destroyed them all.* [30] *Even so will it be in the day when the Son of Man is revealed".*

- Luke 17:26-30

Some key points about how God wants to move us forward, having given you this background; what is God's plan to move you forward? What are the key elements going forward?

The key point I want you to note about the way forward is this; how is God addressing this issue of the believers strategically invading the marketplace? The marketplace is not what many of us think it is. The marketplace is not just where the business takes place. The marketplace includes where the business takes place, it includes government, media, education, entertainment industry, even churches. The marketplace includes everything. The question now is; how are we doing in our assignment to reclaim the marketplace as believers?

> *"The marketplace is not what many of us think it is. The marketplace is not just where the business takes place. The marketplace includes where the business takes place, it includes government, media, education, entertainment industry, even churches. The marketplace includes everything"*

FEW POINTS TO NOTE TO BALANCE YOUR UNDERSTANDING:

1.   When God wanted to commission the works of the Tabernacle who did he use to do it?

> *"And Moses said to the children of Israel, "See, the Lord has called by name Bezalel the son of Uri, the son of Hur, of the tribe of Judah; and He has filled him with the Spirit of God, in wisdom and understanding, in knowledge and all manner of workmanship, to design artistic works, to work in gold and silver and bronze, in cutting jewels for setting, in carving wood, and to work in all manner of artistic workmanship. "And He*

*has put in his heart the ability to teach, in him and Aholiab the son of Ahisamach, of the tribe of Dan. He has **filled them with skill** to do all manner of work of the engraver and the designer and the tapestry maker, in blue, purple, and scarlet thread, and fine linen, and of the weaver—those who do every work and those who design artistic works".*

- Exodus 35:30-35 NKJV

The Bible did not say God filled them with anointing. He has filled them with skill. It is very important for us to understand that there is a place for skill acquisition to be able to command value. We must start in the spirit but we must add works to our faith by getting the skill necessary to command value in the marketplace. This is not a contradiction; it is complimentary.

Therefore, it is important that we acquire the right kind of skill. Absolutely crucial. And like I tell people for example; the day the children of Israel left Egypt the economy of Egypt collapsed because they took the silver and gold of Israel with them. But the question is, where did the silver and gold they took come from. It came from the mineral mines in Egypt. Which means all the Egyptians needed to do was just go back to the mines and mine more silver and gold and they will be fine. But what happened is that for the hundreds of years that the Israelites spent in Egypt, the generation of Egyptians that had the skill had all died. So the entire skill of Egypt was with the children of Israel. The day they left Egypt, Egypt's economy had to collapse.

> *"We must start in the spirit but we must add works to our faith by getting the skill necessary to command value in the marketplace"*

Even though they had the raw materials, they could not translate it into anything. It is important for you to understand that when God wanted to build the tabernacle, the very first instruction he gave to Moses was to get this guy who has learnt all these skills from Egypt and bible says *"God filled him with skill"*. So it is important that we get out of this over spirituality many of us hide behind. The purpose of the spiritual is to impact the natural. The real spiritual people are those who impact their environment. So the first point to note is that when God wanted to commission the works of the tabernacle he found men that had skill.

2.   **When God wanted to reveal David to Saul, he used David's skill to do so.** His musical talent or skill was a vehicle God used. Again you see how God used the skill

of David to expose him to the king. His music talent was the vehicle God used first, then later his war skill against Goliath. **Build your skill and package it's value as it could be the vehicle that will reveal you to the world.** Right now you may be in the season of obscurity, God is simply fashioning you.

> *"So he shepherded them according to the **integrity** of his heart, And guided them by the **skillfulness of his hands"**.*
>
> Psalm 78:72 NKJV

> *"It is important that we get out of this over spirituality many of us hide behind. The purpose of the spiritual is to impact the natural. The real spiritual people are those who impact their environment"*

3. **Joseph did not manage Egypt with his dreams; he managed them with skill in humans and resource management.** He wrote a blueprint for his generation on how to manage people. His dream opened the door yes but his skill allowed him to manage Egypt. We need to understand this as believers; you cannot replace the need for skill in certain areas if you are to command value. Please note that skill is not the same thing as academic

qualification. So don't ever equate skill with education. They are not the same thing. Many of the most unskilled people I have met in a place like Nigeria have academic qualifications. Don't equate the two at all, it depends on what the skill is.

> *"His dream opened the door yes but his skill allowed him to manage Egypt"*

4.   Daniel with all his clout and spiritual power was in administration in Babylon. The Bible says he even spoke to the king concerning the three Hebrew children. What did he do? He spoke to the king and as a result of his recommendation; they were appointed into administrative posts in Babylon. It is important for you to understand that though many might remember Daniel for the lion's den encounter and all the other victories, which are true; but he was also a very good administrator as well.

> *"Please note that skill is not the same thing as academic qualification. So don't ever equate skill with education"*

CHAPTER 10

Creating Value Through Strategic Positioning

Now that we have laid those backgrounds, the question now is, how do we position ourselves for this wealth transfer? And as I was meditating about this, the story that the Lord wants me to use to bring this out to you is a story that many of us are familiar with; this is the story of Zacchaeus in the Bible, in Luke 19. Somebody said; "if your ship does not come to you, you can swim and go and meet it". In life there will be two categories of people you will encounter; those that are waiting for their ship to come and meet them and those that will actually go and meet the ship wherever it is.

The story of Zacchaeus in Luke 19 presents leadership and management principles on how to create a positive environment that attracts value and opportunity in your life. Zacchaeus typifies the best way to attract opportunity through what I call strategic positioning. For those of you who might want some background, Zacchaeus was a Jericho based tax collector who was excited about the opportunity to meet Jesus. But he was constrained by his diminutive stature. And when the bible says you are short I am sure you are really short. He therefore decided that he was going to do something to mitigate his disadvantage; but what did he do. He did three things that I want us to look at quickly.

He did three things, which if any of you do that, it will differentiate you instantly in any work of life that you are in. In Luke 19:4 the bible says *"and Zacchaeus ran ahead and climbed up into a sycamore tree to see Jesus".* He realised that Jesus was going to pass that way, so he ran ahead, climbed up a tree to see Jesus. In any competitive arena, be it business, education or any corporate life, you need to have strategic advantage in order to take hold of the opportunities that will come your way. The crowd that were around Jesus was big, the problem Zacchaeus had was that every other person around him were taller than he was. So he could not even see what was going on, not to talk of attracting Christ's attention.

"In life there will be two categories of people you will encounter; those that are waiting for their ship to come and meet

*them and those that will actually go and
meet the ship wherever it is"*

Many others wanted the same opportunity Zacchaeus sought. Tell me which business opportunity do you want to go into right now that others are not interested in the same business. So other people want the same opportunity you seek. Other people want to do the same kind of business you want to do. So like Zacchaeus you may feel that you are at a disadvantage. So what do you do? It is either you give up and say; *I'm lost. Everybody around me has two PhDs and I barely have a first degree. So I am completely at a disadvantage, so I give up and I am going home.* Or you do what Zacchaeus did, understanding that there are things you can do to move forward.

The fact that Zacchaeus managed to get Jesus, not only to see him like others but also to come and stay in his house, which is beyond what other did or got, speaks volumes about how you prevail in a competitive environment. It shows that you are not just able to overtake; you are able to recover all. You are not just to do as well as your competitors; you are supposed to surpass them. That is what Zacchaeus is saying. The very first thing he did was to anticipate.

Let us consider insight of two things Zacchaeus did;

1.   In other to overcome your limitation and competition, and attract the right opportunities, you need to first of all **ANTICIPATE**. That means being able to pre-empt what doors are likely to open next, what goods and services will soon be in demand, what jobs or business openings are coming up, or what skills or abilities may be needed in the emerging economy. You need to consciously learn how to anticipate what is about to happen. The scripture is full of people who did that. The first battle recorded in scripture is Abraham going to the battle of the kings. Something struck me by that story, the bible says that after Abraham heard that his cousin has been taken captive by the kings and he was going to go into battle with the kings. The bible says and Abraham took the trained men of war with him. Question, since there has never been a battle, or any war before that time, how did he have trained men of war? There was no war recorded before that time, yet Abraham had trained men of war. Which meant what, he prepared for war in time of peace. **He anticipated what was going to happen**, he may never need them but he said let me just train them anyway.

In other words it is better to have what you don't need than to need what you don't have. You need to learn to anticipate, because if you don't anticipate, the slots would have all gone by the time you wake up. That is what

Zacchaeus did. Because he knew which road Jesus was to pass on, imagine what would have happened if he had run ahead and climbed the tree on the wrong road. For him to have done that it seemed that there are two possible ways; it is either he has observed Jesus make that journey before and realized that it is always the road he takes or he has worked out the permutation so that there is no other way he could take given the size of the crowd around him and all that.

"You need to consciously learn how to anticipate what is about to happen"

He must have done some exercise, some studying to understand that this is the road for a certain. Anticipation gives you the head start that allows you to undertake strategic assessment needed, and the by the time you are done, other people are still sleeping. You need to learn to anticipate. I was reading a technical magazine few months ago and there is this guy in California in the US that hacked into iPhone 4S and he was able to get the iPhone to take panoramic pictures. When Apple heard about this, they were very angry; later on they confirmed that it was a feature embedded in the iPhone 4S that has not yet been enabled. Rumours had it that it was meant to be part of iPhone 5 'new' features. In other words, they had anticipated what will be needed in the future and have prepared for iPhone 5 features while releasing iPhone 4S. They know where the direction of the travel is. What this guy did was to run ahead of them as it were, by enabling this hidden feature. One of the things that keep Apple innovative is that they are always a step ahead. So it is important for you to understand you need to learn to anticipate if you are to command value.

> *"Anticipation gives you the head start that allows you to undertake strategic assessment needed, and the by the time you are done, other people are still sleeping"*

2.   The second thing Zacchaeus did was that he **RAN AHEAD**. If you are anticipating you can anticipate all you like but if you still sit with the crowd, it is not going to work. Running ahead involves separating yourself from the congested place of competition. In the business arena, running ahead speaks of differentiation, which is about specialising or creating a unique identity for your business, your company or your ministry. It involves doing things differently from everyone else in the same industry that will be noticed. And also being able to attract clientele that find your service proposition uniquely attractive. You need to understand that the shallow end of every river is

always crowded. And you don't catch much fish there. You need to go into the deep.

"Running ahead involves separating yourself from the congested place of competition"

DEVELOPING A PERSONAL BRAND

For a prospective employee, employer, business owner, or whatever it is you are; one of the ways you differentiate yourself is through what I call personal branding. **A brand is an accumulation of words, thoughts, images and emotions that come to mind when people think or hear or see your touch or experience a person.** So your personal brand therefore is not what you say it is, it is what people think or say it is.

A lot of it has to do with perception, how you are perceived. Remember the widow look at the man of God and said I perceived you are a prophet. How did she perceive, there is a way he conducted himself, there is a way he spoke. Remember the woman by the well when she encountered Jesus; again she knew that somebody telling me all these things cannot just be an ordinary guy, so again through certain characteristics she perceived. So the key question is: Why the need for personal branding for believers when we are supposed to live by favour? The just shall live by faith, so I don't need to brand anything you may say. I can just do anything I like; the favour of God will make the difference.

> *"You need to understand that the shallow*
> *end of every river is always crowded. And*
> *you don't catch much fish there. You*
> *need to go into the deep"*

Now that is true but let me explain something to you. God is the source of all knowledge we agree. Therefore no advances in medicine, science will take place without God's permission. When I asked the Lord the question this is the answer He gave me. He says *"son in the absence of my specific divine instruction to go an exceptional or unusual route, you must follow established principles because I gave them in the first place"*.

For instance, God has told you He needs you to build him a physical house. God can give you a vision and ideas of a new structural engineering method and principle to build a house nobody has built before but if God does not give you that; follow the normal structural engineering laws to make your building stand. In the absence of specific divine instruction that leads to deviation, you must follow established principles because those laws and knowledge were established by God in the first place.

> *"Your personal brand therefore is not what you say it is, it is what people think or say it is"*

As another example; you wake up one day and got this divine visitation that God want you to be a musician, but you don't know how to play instrument; two things can happen. It is possible that God can give you a divine encounter and enablement and in 24 hours you will be playing like a pro. It is possible, but highly unlikely, because most likely you will then need to learn how to play instruments. In other words, whenever you want to make a decision, you need to ask; "Lord what are you saying about this?" If you don't get the specific divine instruction to do something exoteric, completely different, or given unique insight into a particular thing, what God is trying to say is that "Look there is known knowledge out there; use it". That is why you need to understand that branding is important. What am I saying? Let me give you a practical example.

> *"In the absence of specific divine instruction that leads to deviation, you*

*must follow established principles
because those laws and knowledge were
established by God in the first place"*

ELEMENTS OF PERSONAL BRANDING

What are the few elements of personal branding? If you
are talking about branding yourself personally, what are
some of the things that can set you apart as a person in
terms of branding yourself?

1.   YOUR VALUES AND YOUR CHARACTER.
Sometimes when your values and character are in play;
initially it looks like a disadvantage. But the people who
are seeing it are making a note of it. They know what they
should bring your way and what they should not bring
your way. Don't think that joining them is always the right
way to go. Some people will tell you, you want business; go
to this guy. Why? He is as honest as they come. Many
times when you have encountered that person, his honesty
has been his advantage, but each time, you were making
note that this guy is so honest and happy to take it as a
disadvantage if need be. So when there is a business that
needs honesty, you quickly bring it his way. It is therefore
important for you to note that values and character can
define you.

2.   YOUR TALENT OR YOUR SKILL: This is

straight forward enough. Your dominant skill or talent can brand you. It happens everyday.

3. YOUR PERSONAL MISSION: What has become an obsession can define you in such a way that anytime somebody thinks about that particular topic or issue, it is you they will think about. Because you have pounded it into their head repeatedly that it is your mission in life.

4. UNIQUE KNOWLEDGE: can be a differentiation. You might have a knowledge that is so rare about something that can make you different. That can become your personal branding element.

5. COMMUNICATION SKILL: If Barak Obama is not the President of the United States; his personal brand will revolve mainly around his communication and oratory skills. Somebody once said about a salesman; *"this guy is so good that he can sell car to the dead".* That shows how good that person is if the dead can buy cars from him. But the logic more or less is that he is very good. In sales they will tell you that there are three types of customer; there is a customer that will tell you (if you are a car dealer for example) I want a Volkswagen, V8, they will tell you all the technical parameters he desires; don't bother selling too much to such as he know exactly what he wants, just give him the key to the car. For the second category; they just want a car. It may be a VW, Ford or Audi, but they don't know the spec, those are the ones you can be sold to easily. There is a third category and they are those who didn't think they need a car in the first place. But will end up leaving with a car, because by the time you finish with them, you will make them to need what they didn't think they needed. It is important you understand that communication skill is very vital.

I often tell people that the fact that they have spoken does not mean they have been understood. You have not communicated until you have been understood. Many of us because we open our mouths to say something, we think people should understand us. That is why five people can hear the same thing and give you five different versions. Because every time you are hearing things, you are filtering it through your own experiences, prejudices, preconceptions; you are filtering those things through the prism of those residual facts. And therefore it can shape what you have heard. So it is your job to make sure that you are really understood.

So the way and quality with which you speak can become part of your personal brand. You can be famous for the way you speak.

6.   DRESS SENSE OR ETIQUETTE: Appearance and presentation are keys to getting attention in the competitive market place. The way you dress and present yourself can easily become part of your personal brand. You can determine the kind of first impressions people have of you by the way you dress and present yourself. This is what dress code is all about.

> *"The way and quality with which you speak can become part of your personal brand. You can be famous for the way you speak"*

7.   Social Networking Position. Given the increasing dominance of Social Networks; especially among the youth; your social network position can become an element of personal branding. You can then leverage such dominance to create value that will fuel your personal brand.

CHAPTER 11

Signs of Loss
of Value As An Employee

The truth is that entrepreneurship is a tool for biblical wealth transfer. There is always going to be a limit to what you can earn as a salaried person. Now that does not mean that it is wrong to be on salary. It means that when you are on salary, you have to learn how to distinguish yourself and get to the top. Things are changing so much in the current economic climate and we need to understand what the signs are that your career is at risk.

What are the signs to look out for? You are working in an office, you have beaten the signs of redundancy now and then, and many will fast and pray, that redundancy will not reach them. It is good to fast and pray. But as we go through these signs, you will see that there are some things that indicate to you that even if God was your employer, God will fire you Himself. It is important that there are some things that you have to watch out for as an employee; to remain relevant.

What are the signs that your career is at risk, because things in life are constantly moving and life itself is in constant motion. And you need to understand whether you are moving with time or you are still buried where you are. The most successful people in life consistently transform their economic fortunes by strategic positioning, the acquisition of relevant knowledge and speedy response to opportunities.

However, some individuals significantly disable themselves from this process through their career choices and economic positioning. These are people with limited options who run the risk of being marginalised by the dynamic and evolving knowledge economy. Believe it or not, you are under threat of career stagnation or extinction if:

1. **Your career prospects are only tied to your current job.** Some people are only suitable for a particular job in a particular company. They have a narrow set of skills and abilities that make it impossible for them to be employed elsewhere. They therefore hang on to their jobs as if their very lives depend on them. You must be good enough to be employed at the same or even a higher level if

you had to leave your current job or if your organisation closed down. You are at risk if you lack the capacity to rebuild your career outside your current job. I have seen people who have been in management before who find themselves unemployed for long periods because they failed to broaden their scope of relevance.

"The most successful people in life consistently transform their economic fortunes by strategic positioning, the acquisition of relevant knowledge and speedy response to opportunities"

2.   **Your career success is dependent on a person.** Some people are surviving in organisations not on merit but by virtue of the fact that they are in the good books or related to someone in a position of authority. That is not the right way to build one's career. Should that person suddenly leave the business or change their opinion of you, it could mark a certain decline or stagnation for you.

"You are at risk if you lack the capacity to rebuild your career outside your current job"

3.   **You only have the minimum qualification for**

your job. Sometime ago, certain positions in corporate organisations were filled by people with O-Level and A-Level qualifications. Things have since changed and today, many of those hitherto-mundane roles are occupied by university graduates. Similarly, some positions previously held by graduates are now being offered to post-graduate applicants. You may still hold such a position by dint of hard work and long service even though you have a lower qualification. However, you must not be comfortable there: you are at risk because you will most likely be the first to go if the company ever needs to cut its staff numbers. In that case, your options will be very limited because after leaving the organisation, you are not likely to find the same job or level elsewhere.

4.   **You have only one dimension of skill.** Our dynamic world keeps changing every day and the knowledge and skills we have and work with are continuously becoming obsolete. If you have only one dimension of the critical skill you require for your work you are in trouble. Imagine someone who types excellently on the typewriter but cannot use a computer. That is a limited dimension of the typing skill that could easily render the person redundant. The same thing applies to people who get stuck on one machine or only one model of the key machine used in their work. The rapid rate of change in technology implies that you must update

yourself and consistently keep abreast in order to retain the same position. If you refuse to upgrade yourself or migrate to newer models of the machines you work with, you reduce your chances of earning more and growing in your organisation. Do not leave things to chance. Start improving your skills today.

5. **You can be replaced by someone more competent at a lower cost.** What would you do as an employer if someone with a low competence level wants to get paid more and you are aware of better and cheaper alternatives? That is the challenge facing many people today. They are not at the cutting edge of their fields but are sadly unaware or unconcerned about it. There has been a lot of lobbying in the USA because competent Information Technology (IT) professionals from India are available for half the price of their American counterparts and are thus knocking them out of business. Incidentally, the hue and cry that led to the unfortunate xenophobic attacks in South Africa in 2008 were partly because migrant workers from other African countries were alleged to be offering better service at lower cost to employers and thus marginalising the locals.

> *"If you have only one dimension of the critical skill you require for your work you are in trouble"*

You are at risk if your potential employer can find more competent and cheaper alternatives not just from your country but from any part of the world. Globalisation has made it possible for organisations to look anywhere in the world for the skills they need. Your competition is therefore no longer restricted to your geographical jurisdiction.

6.   You can easily be replaced by a machine. With rising costs of labour especially in more advanced economies, technologies and machines are consistently being designed to significantly reduce the number of people who operate them. This trend means that future production processes will become more integrated and require significantly less hands. As a result, unskilled workers in many fields will find themselves competing with machines for their jobs. And considering that machines do not come with all the human resource costs and uncertainties that come with employing people, the natural consequence is marginalisation and displacement of such people.

> *"You are at risk if your potential employer can find more competent and cheaper alternatives not just from your country but from any part of the world"*

7.   **You are functionally illiterate.** Formal education opens one up to the world and lays a foundation on which other educational structures must be built. One cannot possibly acquire all the knowledge one needs for career success from the classroom. Indeed, people often study subjects in school that have little or no direct relevance to the industries in which they operate. One could therefore conclude that the primary role of educational qualification is to open the career door. After entry, there is no point flaunting the degree because qualifications by themselves do not solve the problems that plague organisations on a daily basis. What really makes a difference is the industry-specific or relevant knowledge that you acquire along the way either at school, through courses and seminars or by careful observation, reading and personal study. If you are not appropriately informed or educated about the work you do and the industry in which you operate, you are likely to be marginalised as your company continues to grow and the marketplace becomes more competitive.

8.   **You cannot survive six months without working.** One of the easiest ways to measure financial independence is the ability of the individual to live a normal life for six months if for some reason they find themselves out of work or unable to earn an income. If you have not invested to the point where your stocks or

assets can tide you over a six-month period, your career progress could easily be derailed by circumstances. While speaking in a conference in the United States, we met a young man who had lost everything because he suffered a domestic accident that left him bedridden for three months and unable to work. His first challenge was that he was uninsured: that meant he got no compensation for his injuries. Subsequently, he also lost his job and ended up at home for the most part of that year. He suddenly found himself unable to pay his mortgage and bills. At the time we met him, his home was being foreclosed while his cars had been repossessed. From a well-paying job and comfortable conditions, the guy found himself unemployed and almost homeless within a short space of time.

> *"What really makes a difference is the industry-specific or relevant knowledge that you acquire along the way either at school, through courses and seminars or by careful observation, reading and personal study"*

9.   You do not have what it takes to make it in another country. If you lack the talent, language or skills to earn a living in any other country than the one you are living and working in, you could also be at risk. In today's globalised economy, you could find yourself having to live in another country when you did not plan for it. Political instability in parts of the world has made this a reality for many. Alternatively, opportunities related to your field could open so wide in another country that it would be imperative for you to work there for a while to advance your career. If your knowledge, skills and experience are so local that they are not relevant abroad, you deny yourself the chance to participate. Moreover, if you are only a vernacular speaker and cannot communicate in any international language, you are likely to further reduce your options.

"If you have not invested to the point where your stocks or assets can tide you over a six-month period, your career progress could easily be derailed by circumstances"

10.   You are forgetful, careless and lack attention to detail. Information is an important currency for personal and organisational development. In most job assignments, one of the most critical requirements for success is the ability to observe, assimilate, store or retrieve relevant information when needed. If you are forgetful or careless, you could easily ignore or mishandle important data and thus restrict your career progress. Information is about fine details. Sometimes one misplaced dot or comma can totally distort the value or meaning of an important business transaction. If you are not detail-oriented and are in the habit of making careless mistakes, you will never be a favourite with any boss and are likely to suffer career stagnation

> *"If your knowledge, skills and experience are so local that they are not relevant abroad, you deny yourself the chance to participate"*

We live in a constantly changing world. 31 billion questions are asked on Google every month. With over 750Million subscribers, Facebook would have been the world's third most populous country if it were one. Social networks are the most dominant activity on the Internet and have redefined the face of communication and business the world over. In the face of rapid changes, globalisation and increased competition, individuals who are not equipped with requisite knowledge, skills, competence and versatility will find themselves becoming dinosaurs in the 21st Century.

"If you are not detail-oriented and are in the habit of making careless mistakes, you will never be a favourite with any boss and are likely to suffer career stagnation"

CHAPTER 12

Creating Value
Through New Business Ideas

Essential part of strategic positioning in the marketplace and commanding value is knowing how to generate valuable Business ideas. Ideas rule the world. Look around you; everything you see was once an idea in somebody's head. There are many things that are real today; that were once simply ideas. Reality is a product of ideas that was acted upon. You are just one idea away from your breakthrough; One idea away from abundant riches. On daily basis lots of ideas come to you; but what can you do about it?

12 WAYS TO GENERATE BUSINESS IDEAS

1.   ADD VALUE OR ADDITIONAL BENEFIT TO AN EXISTING PRODUCT; AND SELL AT THE

SAME PRICE AS THE OLD VERSION OR LESS.

You will be amazed at how many people have been waiting for the added value you have included. On a trip to the US few years ago, I saw a bottle of oxygenated water. This is like any other bottle water but with added oxygen. The producers simply added an extra benefit to an existing product.

2.   TAKE AN ORDINARY PRODUCT; THEN STRIP IT TO ITS BASICS AND OFFER THE SUBSTANCE OF IT AND SELL AT A VERY CHEAP PRICE IF POSSIBLE.

For instance in Europe there is Ryanair. The company is successful; because they stripped the product to its basics (Flying) and then offered it at a cheaper price; without the frills. The basic substance here is flying.

3.   ADD OR REMOVE PACKAGING FROM AN EXISITING PRODUCT OR SERVICE.

Ask yourself; *What are the products out there that can generate a new market if packaged properly or differently.*

There are products that will become more functional if packaged differently. For instance; while most people like lovely looking laptops; a market was created for rough and rugged (and ugly looking) laptops for use in war zones and in the field. That is how packaging was used to create a new market for an existing product. So look into your community, your supermarkets <u>and stores</u>, and you will see products that can be re-packaged for new success.

Also, THERE ARE SOME PRODUCTS THAT ARE PACKAGED TOO MUCH. If 30% of the cost of a product is packaging; then you can instantly create a market for the same product with little or no packaging offered at a cheaper price. E.G; Outlet perfume shops in the US. They sell many without the original box packaging but at about 25% cheaper than its regular price.

4.   PACKAGE SOMETHING MADE EASY OR COMBINATION OF PRODUCT.

For instance, in the early days, we had tea, coffee, chocolate sold as stand-alone products. You then need to add milk and sugar and water. But companies later got new ideas by selling Ready-Made versions. There are chocolate drinks with sugar and milk already included. So all you need is water; thus saving you the need to buy sugar and milk. This easy version creates new market and expands existing ones.

Same with Yam Powder for Pounded Yam. It is Pounded Yam made easy. Same with ready-made salad mix. Saves you cutting the items individually. So what can you make easy for others that can generate money. Think deeply.

5.   ADD "SPEED OF DELIVERY" TO BASIC PRODUCT OR SERVICE AND OFFER TO PEOPLE.

People are willing to pay more for speed. People will pay more for a letter that will be delivered in 24hrs rather than wait for 7days. That is how DHL was born. Look at services or product that already exist; see if you can add speed of delivery to add value.

6.   USE DESIGN OR PACKAGING TO ENHANCE A BASIC APPLIANCE OR PRODUCT.

There are products that certain people do not buy because it looks cheaply packaged or without class. If you repackage the same product in a stylish way; new market could be created. For instance there are Bottled water for 50p and there are others for £3 or more. What is the main difference: Packaging. For example, Children snickers, shoes with lights when you walk. New market for existing product.

7.   USE DESIGN TO OFFER PRODUCT THAT RELIEF STRESS.

Life is full of stress sources. This is why Massage products sell very well for instance. If you have ever been stressed; ask yourself, what product or service could have offered you relief from that stress. You may be on to something new.

8. GENERALISE A HORDED OR SCARCE TECHNOLOGY OR IDEA.

Help bring obscure product or services to the mainstream; and make money in the process. There are lots of products out there today that are offshoots of Nasa hidden experiments. What skill do you have? Can you speak German or Russian? Offer the service and make money in the process. Start a language school.

9. OFFER BETTER VALUE BY COMBINING ATTRIBUTES.

For example, **Business mobile phones**. Traditionally, when people travel they carry around a phone, a calculator, a radio, a diary, a voice recorder, a calendar etc. **So a new generation of phones were developed that combines all these and more.** This is how to combine attributes; thus offering better value. Look for related products and see how they can be combined into a new single product.

10. LOOK FOR A NEED AND FILL IT.

If there is a need; there is a market. Be observant and see needs that need filling. My experience with on-the-spot photographers at a wedding in Nigeria was that they filled a need for people to take home a record of them well dressed at a party.

11.   SOLVE PROBLEMS FOR PEOPLE

Solving problems can bring wealth. Look into what problems you and people have. See how you can solve them.

12.   BRING OUT INSPIRATIONAL OR CREATIVE PRODUCTS

If you have ideas that can inspire others; package it and offer it to others. Write them down; bring out books. Produce CDs or DVDs that can inspire and help others. Pastors, Teachers, this is your terrain.

The New Rules of Money

To be able to command value; you also have to understand how money works. So what are the new rules of money. The old rules have changed. For any of you who understand how the system works, you will understand that rules are constantly changing. What was ok before may not be ok now. So there are new rules of money. You need to understand these things in order to know how to command financial value.

1. The first new rule of money is that **KNOWLEDGE IS THE NEW MONEY**. The paper in your hand is no longer money. If you are not informed, you will be deformed. Information is the new currency. If you are not inspired like somebody said, you will expire. It is the currency of the future, the empire of the mind. Knowledge is the new currency. The paper money is not

the only medium of exchange. For those of you who know the history of money know that it has not always been paper. There have been different ways the world had been trading, but the future belongs to those who know. And those who know will dominate those that don't know. So equip yourself with the right knowledge.

2.   The second new rule of money is that **YOU MUST LEARN HOW TO USE DEBT SUCCESSFULLY.** What do I mean? Unlike how you have been thought before, not all debt is bad in the real economy. You must learn to use debt. In my book out there called "no more debt", one of the chapters in it talked about people coming out of debt. One of the first thing I mentioned there is that there is nowhere in the Bible that it said that borrowing is a sin. In fact, if borrowing is a sin, then God is an accessory to a crime. Why? Because he said that *you shall lend to many nations, you will not borrow.* So if borrowing is a sin, why would God say we should lend? If borrowing is a sin, then God will not ask us to lend because he would be asking us to help people to sin.

But the problem is that you have to learn how to use debt. There are two types of debt; Good debt and bad debt. The bad or wrong debt is money borrowed for consumption. You borrow money for holiday, you borrow money to buy car, borrow money to buy TV, all those things; money that you borrow for things you consume is wrong debt.

"There have been different ways the world had been trading, but the future belongs to those who know. And those who know will dominate those that don't know. So equip yourself with the right knowledge"

The good debt can be for leverage and not a problem, money acquired for investments and certain business opportunities. For example, for financial and tax purposes, if British Airways has one billion pound in their account today cash, and they need to buy five new planes for say five hundred million pounds, in which case they could easily write a cheque for five hundred million. How many of you know that British Airways will never write a cheque for five hundred million to buy those planes? Because it is a wrong way of spending money. What will they do? They will lease the planes for five hundred million; maybe for seven per cent per annum interest. But their own five hundred million they will put in an investment that can yield twenty per cent per annum. Even though they have leased the plane, the money they have now invested is yielding more as an investment. And they are paying off the lease, and more importantly, they have left over. This thing also has a tax advantage over buying it out rightly. In that kind of situation, British Airways is in debt, but it is not a bad debt.

You need to learn how to use debt. And if you are the type that clear your credit card account fully monthly; (one of the things my wife is disciplined at, is paying off her credit card in full at the end of the month); you are using debt appropriately. If you have that kind of discipline; for example even a credit card from the consumption point of view can be used positively. Because that is fifty days free money as you don't have to pay instantly.

It is important for us to understand that we should not be dogmatic about it and think anything debt is all bad. In business by and large, you cannot survive in business without some form of credit facility. What do I mean? Your supplier gives you supplies_and invoices you thirty days later, that is debt until you pay it off. You need to know how to use money. It is called other peoples' money and you need to understand how to use other peoples' money as leverage.

3.   You must learn how to **CONTROL YOUR CASH FLOW.** You have to learn how to control the cash that comes into your hand. For every money you make, there are overheads that you must account for. One of the things

that will surprise some of you is that I meet some people in business who thinks that turnover is same as profit. One of them will say, "Yeah, I have made a thousand pounds". And I will say, "no you have not". This is how many Christian businesses fail. You have not made a thousand pounds, what was your cost of delivering that service. Until you take your cost out and then the difference is identified as your profit. You have not made a thousand pounds. What many people do is that they will take that one thousand pounds as profit and suddenly finds out that the business is not making it. The reason is because you are not replenishing all the inputs into making that money. You have to learn to control you cash flow. I tell people that if your outgoings exceed your incoming, your upkeep will become you downfall. So you need to learn to balance that.

We tell people "spend within your means" and I tell people that you need to be careful about that statement. If you are in debt and you are just trying to sort out you finances, please spend within your means. But if you want to make that a philosophy for the rest of your life, then you will remain in poverty. You have to expand; you have to learn how to stretch out of your comfort zone. And that won't happen if you are constantly saying that everything has to be within your means. Controlling your cash flow helps you to create value.

4.　　The fourth new rule of money is; **PREPARE FOR BAD TIMES AND YOU WILL ALWAYS HAVE GOOD TIMES.** In Egypt, the seven years of famine was prepared for in the seven years of plenty. The future belongs to those who prepare for it. You need to understand that wealth and economics are in circle. Prior to 1960 before Bernard Keynes brought out his theory, the world was constantly going into recession almost every twenty years or there about. So there is a cycle to world economy. And of course what he suggested was ways of mitigating the downturn by using public expenditure as he called it to increase the cash flow in the economy and keep the economy going until it is able to grow again. I think the good term for it now is called the "bailout"; Public sector funding etc. The point I am making is economy is a cycle and you have to prepare for bad times always so that you will have good times. Remember like I said earlier about preparing for war in the time of peace.

> *"If you are in debt and you are just trying to sort out you finances, please spend within your means. But if you want to make that a philosophy for the rest of your life, then you will remain in poverty"*

5.   UNDERSTAND THE NEED FOR SPEED.

Speed is a key money generator in our current economic climate. The nature of the world of digital economics is that everybody wants everything fast. That is why in the last decade the consumption of microwaved food has gone up exponentially. Everybody wants everything done instantly. If you are slow, people don't want to reckoned with you. We are dealing with a microwave generation. Anything that cuts delay and speed up production and delivery is a guaranteed money generator. Speed is of essence. It does not matter how good you are with what you do, if speed is not there people carry their businesses elsewhere.

There is nothing you do that is exclusive to only you in this world. Therefore your differentiation is your speed. That is why fast foods make money. McDonalds don't make hamburgers for everybody; they make hamburgers for people in a hurry. It is important you understand that speed is of essence. In whatever you do, it is what differentiates you; it is why you make money. Speed can enable you to command value.

6.   YOU NEED TO LEARN THE LANGUAGE OF MONEY.

Every profession has its language. I remember a few years ago, I woke up one day and God told me I know that you have so many skills already. But for where I am taking you next, one of the skills you have to acquire is legal skills. I said ah! After everything I do, with all my schedule how am I going to cope? God said that is what you must do to prepare yourself for the new season ahead. So I went to register in a University to study law part time. One of the things I have learnt so far is that in law you develop a complete new language. Words that you think mean something to you could mean different things to lawyers. Doctors will be speaking to each other and you will not understand a word of what they are saying. Every profession has its language.

So you need to learn the language of money. If you must spend time and invest in learning about money, you must do so to be in the flow. You need to read books, go to seminars. Money speaks. And money is attracted to those who understand its language. You have to learn to speak the language of money. It is also about understanding about how money works. You need to understand that the system out there in terms of the banks, the government, whichever country you are in, the government taxations system, they are all rigged against you. They are not there to help you per se. Banks are not there to help you. That is why somebody said a banker is somebody who gives you umbrella when it is sunny and when it is raining he takes it away.

It is important you understand that the system out there is not fair. And if you don't understand the language of money, you will always be singing the song of victims. There are people you meet, they complain about their banks; they complain about tax, they complain about everything. And you ask; why are you complaining about everything. You need to understand that these things were not setup to favour you. It is you that should know their language and know how to navigate your way around it lawfully and successfully.

"Anything that cuts delay and speed up production and delivery is a guaranteed money generator"

7. **LIFE IS A TEAM SPORT, SO YOU NEED TO CHOOSE YOUR OWN TEAM.** In other words, the days of lone rangers are gone. The rich people today work with other people as a team. Nobody is wealthy as a solo player. You cannot make it alone. There are specific people you need. And one of the things is this, the best financial advice I was ever given, was given by somebody who told me so many years ago; "…if you have to get an advice, make sure you pay for it". I did not understand the value then. In an atmosphere where believers are used to "free" everything you can see the challenge of this counsel. But nothing is free, somebody is paying for it if not you. This is a major psychological barrier in the church today; this issue of everything has to be free. It is affecting the church because people are not willing to pay for what will change their lives. As a businessperson therefore, you have to understand that it is a team sport.

> *"You need to read books, go to seminars.*
> *Money speaks. And money is attracted to*
> *those who understand its language"*

8.   YOU MUST LEARN HOW TO PRINT YOUR OWN MONEY. If knowledge is the new money, then produce your own product. Write that book you have been talking about. Start that idea you are supposed to start. Printing cash is illegal but you must learn how to produce things that can print money for you. Every time that you produce a product or service, you are printing money. When you write a book and put it for sale, you are printing money. When you add value to the lives of other people, you are also printing money. The question is when was the last time you printed money? Think about that for a second, because if you don't do that, you will not come into a place that you need to be.

"The rich people today work with other people as a team. Nobody is wealthy as a solo player. You cannot make it alone. There are specific people you need"

CHAPTER 14

Get Ready...
Get Ready...Get Ready

Opportunity is a haughty goddess who wastes no time with those who are unprepared.

- George Clason

1 "Then the kingdom of heaven shall be likened to ten virgins who took their lamps and went out to meet the bridegroom. 2 Now five of them were wise, and five were foolish. 3 Those who were foolish took their lamps and took no oil with them, 4 but the wise took oil in their vessels with their lamps. 5 But while the bridegroom was delayed, they all slumbered and slept."6 "And at midnight a cry was heard: 'Behold, the bridegroom is coming; go out to meet him!' 7 Then all those virgins arose and trimmed their lamps. 8 And the foolish said to the wise, 'Give us

some of your oil, for our lamps are going out.' 9
But the wise answered, saying, 'No, lest there
should not be enough for us and you; but go
rather to those who sell, and buy for yourselves.'
10 And while they went to buy, the bridegroom
came, and those who were ready went in with
him to the wedding; and the door was shut. 11
"Afterward the other virgins came also, saying,
'Lord, Lord, open to us!' 12 But he answered and
said, 'Assuredly, I say to you, I do not know you.
- Matthew 25:1-12

The 'Parable of the Wise and Foolish Virgins' as told by Jesus succinctly captures the important correlation between **preparation, timing and opportunity.** Ten virgins were appointed to escort a bridegroom to a wedding ceremony. Their participation hinged on their carrying of burning lamps. Each of them had a lamp as expected. However, while the wise virgins carried extra oil in their vessels to keep the flame burning for a long time, the foolish ones lacked foresight and failed to make adequate provision, thus running out at the moment of truth and being exempted from the feast. The foolish virgins were locked out in the darkness of suffering and anguish while the **five industrious virgins who had enough light went in for the celebration.**

It is interesting to analyse this parable as an allegorical representation of economic opportunities in the 21st Century. The key elements in the parable can, therefore, be interpreted as follows:

The Ten Virgins in the story could be made to represent beginners or people who are ready to move to the next level in the economic marketplace. They could be fresh graduates, start-up entrepreneurs or anyone yearning for a great new future. Virgins could also stand for those who, though lacking in economic experience, have kept themselves in readiness for emerging opportunities. In a broader sense, everyone could be said to be a virgin because there are areas of economic opportunity that each one is yet to explore or experience.

THE BRIDEGROOM is a type of Christ Himself and economically he could be said to represent **THE OPPORTUNITY OF A LIFETIME;** the kind of opening that easily redefines one's economic future. The meeting with the bridegroom is a long-anticipated encounter or appointment with that influential person who could turn things around for you in a big way. This is the kind of opportunity that, when taken, justifies the years of waiting by virtue of the sheer magnitude of blessings it brings. It is a divinely ordained, once-in-a-lifetime encounter for which one must be absolutely ready and prepared.

THE WEDDING FEAST represents the **enjoyment and celebration that result when adequate preparation meets the right opportunity.** It is the benefit that comes from actualising the potential offered by an opportunity. It is the appointment letter that comes when you excel at the interview. It is the contract that is signed when your proposal meets the approval of the evaluating authority. The doors to the wedding feast are only open to those who can demonstrate that they are adequately prepared and have their lamps burning.

THE BURNING LAMP typifies **knowledge and enlightenment.** To have light is to be enlightened, which is **"to be educated, informed, instructed, well-advised or knowledgeable."** An enlightened person has spiritual and intellectual insight into the issues of their time. They can also be said to have a full comprehension of a situation or problem. Spiritual enlightenment connotes "having a spiritual revelation or deep insight into the meaning and purpose of things." That only happens when you communicate with or understand the mind of God concerning the issues that confront you.

"The meeting with the bridegroom is a long-anticipated encounter or appointment with that influential person

who could turn things around for you in a big way"

"Enlighten the people generally, and tyranny and oppression of body and mind will vanish like evil spirits at the dawn of day"

- Thomas Jefferson.

THE OIL. In order to have your **light burning at all times you need to have an adequate supply of oil.**
Oil stands for relevant information and new insights. Your level of enlightenment is accentuated or diminished by the supply of oil in your lamp. For you to be continuously knowledgeable and at the cutting edge of any area of economic activity, you need to be continually updated with new information and fresh insights into the dynamics and emerging trends in that field.

In that regard, oil is like the lubricant that keeps the engine of knowledge running smoothly. As soon as it runs out, the engine malfunctions and is unable to perform the expected role. And if it attempts to continue operating without oil, the entire engine gets destroyed. The challenge for many is the attempt to use dimensions of knowledge acquired many years ago to confront the complicated battles of today.

"The doors to the wedding feast are only open to those who can demonstrate that they are adequately prepared and have their lamps burning"

TYPICAL EXAMPLES OF VIRGINS WITHOUT OIL ARE:

1. Lecturers trying to teach with old lecture notes and outdated theories or illustrations,
2. Political leaders whose models are out of touch with modern day realities of their people or
3. Businesses that rely on the old technology, systems and strategies in the face of rapidly-mutating economic trends.

It is important to note that as soon as your supply of oil runs out, your lamp will fade out and you will be in darkness.

THE DARKNESS. To have no light or be in darkness is to be naïve, uninformed, marginalised and unequipped to comprehend or deal with the issues or problems confronting you. In economic terms, people lacking enlightenment do not appreciate the prevailing light of their times. *In today's dispensation, that would mean that they lack understanding of the dynamics of the information-based economic revolution.*

The term "Dark Ages" was coined in reference to the perceived period of cultural and economic deterioration as well as disruption that took place in Western Europe following the decline of the Roman Empire.

"It is important to note that as soon as your supply of oil runs out, your lamp will fade out and you will be in darkness"

The word, which is derived from the Latin *saeculum obscurum* (or dark age), was used to contrast the "darkness" of the period with earlier and later periods of "light". It is generally used to characterise the bulk of the Middle Ages, from around 450 AD till 1000 AD, as a period of intellectual darkness between the extinguishing of the light of Rome, and the Renaissance or rebirth from the 14th century onwards. Darkness connotes the absence of enlightenment, revelation or knowledge.

"Try to imagine what globalization can possibly mean to the half of humanity that has never made or received a telephone call; to the people of sub-Saharan Africa, who have less internet access than the inhabitants of the borough of Manhattan." Kofi Annan, World Economic Forum at Davos in Switzerland on January 28, 2001

It was said at the time that most Africans lived two hours or more from the nearest telephone. These statistics have significantly changed since then and particularly in the area of mobile telephony. Africa is currently one of the fastest growing markets.

The power of light is evidenced by the fact that it dispels or drives away darkness.

When knowledge comes into any environment, ignorance, marginalisation, disease, poverty, low self-esteem and all related vices give way to education, insight, hope and economic renewal. There are a number of parallels between the lessons of this parable and that of the story of the two men who went to build houses in Matthew 7:24-27. Jesus told this story in His conclusion to the Sermon on the Mount to underscore the importance of obedience to principles.

> *24 "Therefore whoever hears these sayings of Mine, and does them, I will liken him to a wise man who built his house on the rock: 25 and the rain descended, the floods came, and the winds blew and beat on that house; and it did not fall, for it was founded on the rock. 26 "But everyone who hears these sayings of Mine, and does not do them, will be like a foolish man who built his*

> house on the sand: 27 and the rain descended, the
> floods came, and the winds blew and beat on that
> house; and it fell. And great was its fall."

Matthew 7:24-27

As was the case in the parable of the virgins, two behaviours were contrasted: that of a wise man and a foolish man. The wise man chose to build his house upon the rock while the foolish man built his upon the sand. The choice of the kind of house to build was a very important decision.

THE TWO TYPES OF VIRGINS AND THE TWO TYPES OF BUILDERS, Both the wise and the foolish, can be found everywhere today. They are present in every organization and business, and individuals by their actions show themselves to be one or the other. The key-differentiating factor is the level of preparation and enlightenment with which they approach opportunities.

It is essential for anyone seeking to gain and sustain competitive advantage to conduct a thorough self-assessment to determine which type of virgin or builder they are.

CHAPTER 15

After You Command Value…what Next?

A s I conclude, I want to give you some basic principles on how to live a balanced life in a way that will make you partake in what God is doing, make your life glorify God, and make you connected to God's purpose on the earth. Commanding value becomes easier for you as you practice these principles. These principles are:

1. REACH HIGH BUT REMAIN GROUNDED.
God has asked us to believe for big things. I sincerely believe that one of the reasons God has not answered some of our prayers is because we have been asking too small. There are some things that when it happens, we don't need to advertise, before people will know that it is only God that could have done it. You are Lazarus and you are sick and they sent for Jesus and Jesus said if I heal a sick Lazarus, nobody will notice. But if I raise a dead Lazarus,

everybody will notice. So sometimes you need a spectacular difficulty to force the hand of God to answer. So reach high but remain grounded.

Believe God for the biggest thing possible. Let me tell you about some secrets of success in life that I have learnt; every effort is equal. The effort it takes to start a small business or ministry, big business or ministry, in terms of raw effort is exactly the same. The differences are the technicalities or what goes into it. So for many of us, it is not a failure of effort. If it is not a failure of efforts and all efforts are the same, I may as well aim for the biggest possible. Like we say where I come from in Nigeria, if a rule is made and you have to pay for wind, then you don't want the small wind to blow you, you want hurricane. In other words, if all efforts are the same and you have to believe God for something, and the effort to believe Him for 100 pounds is the same thing as the effort to believe Him for one million pounds, it does not cost God more to give me a million pound than to give me a pound.

> *But seek ye **first** the kingdom of God, and his*
> *righteousness; and all these things shall be added*
> *unto you.*
>
> Mat.6:33

So reach high but remain grounded. The Bible says seek ye

first the kingdom of God – the Bible did not say seek ye only. Some people interpret it as seek ye only. Seek ye first the kingdom of God means that there are some things we have to seek as second, third, fourth, fifth and so on. But seek ye first the kingdom, means that once you have sought the kingdom and everything now is from the platform of the kingdom; you can now legitimately seek other things. Seek ye first, not seek ye only. So you have to reach high but remain grounded in the basics and be focused on what is priority (The Kingdom).

2.   RUN FAST BUT STAY IN YOUR TRACK.

From the basic rule of athletics that many of us know, it does not matter how fast you are as a runner, if you cross the lanes, you have lost. So speed is important, but you have to remain focused. One of the things about speed is that you must not allow yourself to be distracted. There is nothing worse than speed and distraction combined together. You have to run fast (understand the need for speed) but remain focused. Don't be distracted. There are some people you meet them in January and they say this is the new business idea God told me to do; you meet them in March the business idea has changed; by the time you meet them in July, they are on their fifth idea; such people are accidents going somewhere to happen.

You need to understand that you need to focus. You need

to be consistent. And what I tell people is that the difference between the light in this room and powerful laser for example is that these lights are exactly the same but the lasers are channelled through a very narrow pathway (focused). That is why lasers can cut through anything.

3. PURSUE THE FUTURE BUT LEARN FROM HISTORY. In other words you need to understand that as you are pursuing the future, you have to learn from those who have been there. The Bible says …and they continued in the apostles' doctrine. You need to understand that it is not everything that has gone before that is bad. Infact, there are a lot of things we need to learn from our predecessors. You need to get mentored. I tell people that mentoring is knowledge without the pain of discovery. You don't have the time to make every mistake on earth. If you say, I must make my mistake myself; you die without achieving anything in life. You have no time in life to make every mistake possible, so you learn from other people's mistake. That is what mentoring is all about. It is important that you pay the price to be mentored. Pursue the future but learn from history, so that you don't repeat the mistakes of history.

4. BE INNOVATIVE BUT HONOUR TRADITION. Do not reinvent the will. You need to know there are some products and services that are culturally sensitive. You have to honour tradition in certain societies you operate in as a businessperson. For example, in the West we have this funny feeling about number thirteen, in fact some buildings deliberately don't name some floors 'thirteenth floor' because of the funny thing about the unluckiness of the number thirteen. Whereas in China, thirteen is the luckiest number, if you do a t-shirt with 13 they will snatch it, 13 is considered to be the luckiest number. So if you have a business operating in the UK and the same business is not trying to operate in China, do you think you can operate the same way? You have to therefore be innovative but you have to honour tradition. You have to understand what it is that makes that society tick. It is not all tradition that is bad. As many as are led by the spirit of God not as many are led by tradition but there is nothing wrong with tradition if the Spirit of God does not tell you otherwise. It is absolutely important that you have to honour tradition, not only culturally sensitive, but to be able to become as productive as you should be.

"You need to get mentored. I tell people that mentoring is knowledge without the pain of discovery"

5. DRIVE GROWTH BUT VALUE PEOPLE.

Don't be a slave master. Do not treat people like they are worthless. One of the books I will advise you to read by Dave Carnegie is called "How to win friends and influence people". I read it a long time ago; but one of the things I remember is how you have to value your workers, how you value people. In the book he said many times he will walk through his factories along with another staff (who knows the names of all the staff). So as he passes people he will great them with their personal names. As he is working round, he (the Chaperon) will whisper to him, that is James and Dave will say *hi James, how are you doing?* Simple things like that excited the staff members and they felt valued that the boss knows their names. Simple things like that made them feel valuable. You have to drive growth but not at the expense of people.

6. THINK BIG BUT LIVE SMALL TO START WITH.

In other words, you are thinking big; you have a massive idea, but don't begin to live big tomorrow because you are thinking big today, if you are not there yet. Think big but live small to start until you can actually live big. In other words, those who think big and don't live small to start with are those who enter big debts, because they now want to live out what they are thinking. It is important that you need to avoid that kind of life to command value.

7. CREATE PROFIT BUT SHARE THE REWARDS. In other words, live generously. Don't pay your staff poorly, don't exploit people. It is implicit in capitalism that you have to exploit people, otherwise you will not have capitalism. There is a law in economics that says "if each means of production is given the value of their commiserate value, the value of their output, the company will go burst". So implied in capitalism means that you can never be paid your worth. So the value of your output is hundred pounds and they give you twenty. The company pockets eighty. For those of you who have worked as consultants, like I did many years, you know how much they charge as your service per day to the client, In my case, it was £2000 per day; but I was only paid £220; the company kept the difference as profits. You can never be paid the value of your output regardless of whom you work for. What differs is weather out of hundred pounds productivity you are paid one pound or forty. But either way you are still never going to get the full value. So as an Christian employer; know that the more you share your profit with your staff the better value your business will have. It is important that you realise that you can never pay your way to do your vision; you can only give your way to fulfil your vision.

8. WIN GLADLY BUT ALSO LOOSE GENEROUSLY. Understand that all things work together for good. Why? Because a defeat can birth your victory journey. You have to loose generously. One of the ways you know children is that children don't loose very well. They don't realise that it is not about winning all the time, the rest of us have to win too. We have to share the winning from time to time. One of the signs of maturity is understanding that you have to learn to loose generously, because a defeat can birth your victory. Sometimes the best times of your life started after a defeat. Think about that. One of my books, I have out there is called "advancement" and in that book I was explaining the story of Joseph. How in the physical, advancement is defined as making upwards progress, but how in God, advancement does not mean that. Because one day Joseph was the top in his father's house, the next day he was down – sold as slave, the following day he was up at the top in Potiphar's house, the next day he was down as a prisoner, the next day he was up in Pharaoh's house.

> *"It is important that you realise that you can never pay your way to do your vision; you can only give your way to fulfil your vision"*

The critical issue is that while he was up he was up and when he was down, he was advancing. In your adversity, you are advancing. You are growing where it matters but you just don't know it. While you have been falsely accused in prison for what you did not do, you are still advancing. Even though if you met Joseph in prison at that time, you would have written him off. Those who have written you off will see. It is important that you understand therefore that your advancement does not stop to take place when you are the top, you are advancing while you are at the top, you are advancing while you are in the valley. It is important that when you are analysing your life, if you are in the valley don't conclude the verdict of your life based on where you are right now.

Because Joseph could have written himself off in prison. But you are advancing whether you are on top or whether you are down because you are growing where it matters. Why? Because God said some things at the mountain top that can only be learnt in the valleys. If you have never been through the valleys, you will never survive in the mountain tops.

9.   **REACH THE WORLD BUT SAVE YOUR HOME.** Make your home a priority. The recent research by Forbes magazine of the top 200 richest people on the planet is interesting. They found out that one of the things that they said contributed to their success and indeed one of the things that is common to all of them, is good home

that allowed them to focus successfully on the business. You cannot succeed well if you don't win in the home front.

> *"If you have never been through the valleys, you will never survive in the mountain tops"*

Books by Charles Omole

1. **Church, Its time to Fly** -- *Learning to fly on Eagles Wing.*

2. **How to Avoid Getting Hurt in Church** -- *13 Steps that will protect you and help create an atmosphere for breakthroughs.*

3. **Must I go to Church** -- *8 Reasons why you must attend Church.*

4. **Freedom from Condemnation** -- *Breaking free from the burden & weight of sin.*

5. **I cannot serve a big God and remain small**

6. **How to start your own business**

7. **How to Make Godly Decisions**

8. **How to avoid financial collapse**

9. **Let Brotherly love continue:** *An insight into love and companionship.*

10. **Breaking out of the debt trap**

11. **Common Causes of Unanswered Prayer.**

12. **How to Argue with God and Win** -- *Biblical strategies on getting God's attention for all your circumstances all of the time*

13. **Avoiding Power Failure** -- *How to generate spiritual power for daily success and victorious living.*

14. **How long should I continue to pray when I don't see an answer?**

OTHER BOOKS BY THE SAME AUTHOR

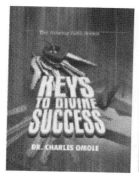

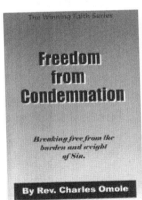

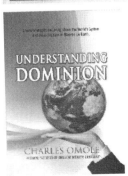

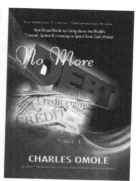

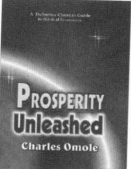

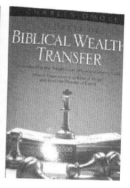

*For more information about our ministry,
world outreaches and a free catalogue of our media
and study materials, please write to:*

Winning Faith Outreach Ministries
151 Mackenzie Road
London. N7 8NF, UNITED KINGDOM

www.charlesomole.com
www.winningfaith.org.uk
www.wisdomforwinning.org

Email: info@Charlesomole.com

Made in the USA
Charleston, SC
06 January 2015